Understand Body Language

Teach® Yourself

Understand Body Language

Gordon R. Wainwright
Revised by Richard Thompson

For UK order enquiries: please contact Bookpoint Ltd, 130 Milton Park, Abingdon, Oxon OX14 4SB. Telephone: +44 (0) 1235 827720. Fax: +44 (0) 1235 400454. Lines are open 09.00–17.00, Monday to Saturday, with a 24-hour message answering service. Details about our titles and how to order are available at www.teachyourself.co.uk

For USA order enquiries: please contact McGraw-Hill Customer Services, PO Box 545, Blacklick, OH 43004-0545, USA. Telephone: 1-800-722-4726. Fax: 1-614-755-5645.

For Canada order enquiries: please contact McGraw-Hill Ryerson Ltd, 300 Water St, Whitby, Ontario L1N 9B6, Canada. Telephone: 905 430 5000. Fax: 905 430 5020.

Long renowned as the authoritative source for self-guided learning – with more than 50 million copies sold worldwide – the **Teach Yourself** series includes over 500 titles in the fields of languages, crafts, hobbies, business, computing and education.

British Library Cataloguing in Publication Data: a catalogue record for this title is available from the British Library.

Library of Congress Catalog Card Number: on file.

First published in UK 1985 by Hodder Education, part of Hachette UK, 338 Euston Road, London NW1 3BH.

First published in US 1985 by The McGraw-Hill Companies, Inc.

This edition published 2010.

Previously published as *Teach Yourself Body Language*.

The **Teach Yourself** name is a registered trade mark of Hodder Headline.

Typeset by MPS Limited, A Macmillan Company.

Printed in Great Britain for Hodder Education, an Hachette UK Company, 338 Euston Road, London NW1 3BH, by CPI Cox & Wyman, Reading, Berkshire RG1 8EX.

The publisher has used its best endeavours to ensure that the URLs for external websites referred to in this book are correct and active at the time of going to press. However, the publisher and the author have no responsibility for the websites and can make no guarantee that a site will remain live or that the content will remain relevant, decent or appropriate.

Hachette UK's policy is to use papers that are natural, renewable and recyclable products and made from wood grown in sustainable forests. The logging and manufacturing processes are expected to conform to the environmental regulations of the country of origin.

Impression number 10 9 8 7 6 5 4 3 2 1

Year   2014 2013 2012 2011 2010

Contents

Introduction

Language is about communication. We tend to think that means *spoken*, but you may be surprised to learn that 90 per cent of what we communicate with each other is *unspoken*, in the form of non-verbal 'signals' we give each other through eye contact, facial expressions, gestures, postures and a variety of sounds and other sensory cues. This is the language of the body. We use it all the time, some of us more effectively than others, and a lot of the time without even realizing we are using it. We start learning it in childhood, just as we learn to speak our own mother tongue by picking up words and meanings from our parents and those around us. But the difference is that while mistakes in our spoken language tend to be corrected, they can be missed, or misinterpreted, in our body language – so you can grow up not realizing you are communicating badly, or ineffectively. Hence the reason for this book.

These signals and cues transmit information about our motives, intentions and feelings. We use the language of the body to convey all kinds of messages and meanings and most of us take this process for granted, never realizing that it takes place at a *sub*conscious, rather than a conscious, level. Just think about it for a minute. Winks, blinks, nods, sighs and grunts – how many of these are you really *aware* of in the process of communication? The point is that language doesn't have to be in the form of words for your meaning to be grasped by someone else. The way you use your body to emphasize or suggest, to inform, illustrate, or even manipulate, is like 'punctuation'. Without it, meaning and emphasis is lost.

You only have to think about the people you most admire, or dislike, to understand the significance of this body talk – the charismatic ones who seem to draw people to them like magnets, the irritating ones who always seem to get in your way, the ones you envy who never seem to put a foot wrong, the quiet ones whose eyes are like rapiers. Something about their physical presence 'talks' to you. Very often the actual words we use to describe behaviour are reflected in our body language. For example, moody people tend to look 'down in the mouth', confident people are said to be 'laid back', assertive people 'reach out', and so forth. Because we're not very good at recognizing the connections between body language and states of mind, we often fail to make the best of ourselves, or the relationships we have with others.

It's only when we look more closely that we begin to reveal things about ourselves and others that we've missed in the course of our busy, everyday lives. If you don't think you are making the best of yourself in personal relationships, at work, or just in your everyday contact with people, the explanations, exercises and experiments at the end of each chapter should help. You probably want to know how to become more skilled in the use of body language and in understanding other people's use of it. A lot of research has been carried out on non-verbal communication over the past few decades in strangely named disciplines like paralinguistics, proxemics, chronemics, kinesics and neurolinguistic programming. But don't worry about the specialist terms, body language isn't rocket science. Improving your communication skills is a combination of common sense, accurate observation, reflection and application. It's a bit like looking at the stars through a telescope for the first time. Things you have missed with the naked eye come sharply into focus – adding definition and meaning to what you have always taken for granted.

So let's get started. First of all, here's a summary of what you will find in each of the forthcoming chapters:

Part one looks at the different situations, or contexts, in which body language plays such an important part in everyday life.

Chapter 1 examines **cultural differences** in the use of body language. We look at the importance of understanding and respecting variations in non-verbal behaviour and examine some of the more unusual, unexpected and significant differences.

Chapter 2 considers the importance of body language in **everyday encounters**, from initial impressions, breaking the ice and small talk, to how we learn to get on with each other and recognize when we are being deceived.

Chapter 3 examines the role of body language in **personal attraction** and considers how non-verbal behaviour can be used to enhance our best assets as well as improve our presentation and relationship skills.

Chapter 4 explores the role of **body language at work** and looks at how self-presentation and performance skills can be enhanced in face-to-face occupations such as nursing, teaching, television interviewing, retail sales and commercial business.

Part two looks in detail at the skills and techniques needed to become a confident body language communicator, and offers an integrated approach to achieving this.

Chapter 5 considers the importance of **eye contact**. A potent form of non-verbal communication, eye contact can be spell-binding, intimidating, informative and central to the making and breaking of relationships. As an indicator of sexual attraction it has no equal. We have to be careful what we are doing with our eyes.

Chapter 6 deals with **facial expressions**. The smile is one of the few universals in body language, as is the 'eyebrow flash' of recognition and greeting. Our faces may not always be our fortunes, but they are certainly where some of the most powerful non-verbal signals originate.

Chapter 7 examines **head talk** – literally the way in which we use our heads to communicate non-verbally. The role of head movements in social interaction is explained and their importance when listening to others is discussed.

Chapter 8 shows how **gestures** and **body movements** are a language in themselves. They 'direct' communication and provide the cues that determine how we relate to each other. Cultural differences in gesture use are also discussed.

Chapter 9 examines the role of **posture** in body language. Once the focus of etiquette and deportment lessons, today posture is seen as a key conveyor of non-verbal signals about our state of mind during communication.

Chapter 10 examines the importance of **personal space** and how we defend it against unwanted invasion through our body language and territorial awareness. How we use **body orientation** to indicate our feelings about people is also discussed.

Chapter 11 deals with **bodily contact** and **touching**. The main distinction between the two is that bodily contact is defined as accidental, whereas touching involves the intention to make physical contact, usually with the hands.

Chapter 12 discusses our obsession with **shape, size** and **looks**. Simple changes to appearance and physique can have a significant effect upon our ability to interact successfully with others.

Chapter 13 considers the importance of **time** and **timing** in our lives and how we synchronize with each other during positive interaction. Making time work for you improves performance and leads to greater self-confidence.

Chapter 14 examines our use of **signals** and **words** and looks at how non-verbal aspects of speech back up, extend and illustrate what we are saying. Pauses, 'ums' and 'ers', pitch, tone, pace and accent are more important than you might suppose.

Chapter 15 considers what **being a success** means and to what extent self-motivation is the key to personal growth and self-improvement.

Hopefully, by the time you reach the end of the book you will understand what body language can do for you in your everyday life and how you can use it to improve your relationships and interactions with others.

Part one
Body language in everyday life

Before we examine the skills and techniques needed to become a confident body language communicator, it's important to recognize some of the everyday life situations, or contexts, in which non-verbal communication plays such a significant role. The chapters that follow will evaluate differences in body language recognition and how we can use this knowledge to enhance our personal and working relationships.

1

Cultural differences

In this chapter you will learn:
- *about cultural differences in the use of body language*
- *how taking account of such differences makes you a more effective communicator.*

Body language is complex enough when you are dealing with people from your own culture, let alone those from other parts of the world where cultural differences may count for a lot in personal and professional communication. Because things can so easily go wrong as a result of misunderstandings or inadvertent mistakes, it may be useful to consider some of the difficulties to be encountered, and how to avoid them.

The world today is a much smaller place than it was even 50 years ago. Travel is relatively easy, and far cheaper than it used to be. We can go to distant places which were once inaccessible to us because of cost, difficult terrain and political boundaries. We watch television pictures from the other side of the globe beamed to us by satellite, chat online thanks to the power of the internet, and text each other on mobile phones from all over the world, at a fraction of the cost it used to be.

The revolution in communications has made all this possible. As a result, the differences between the peoples of the world are diminishing. We know more about each other now than ever before. We share ideas and copy each other's fashions and technical innovations – but we don't always understand how our traditions and customs differ. Just because you can back-pack across China, fly to a conference in Managua, or sleep rough on a Greek holiday beach, doesn't mean you understand or respect the values and uniqueness of the people and places you visit.

Cultural diversity offers huge opportunities for learning about, and integrating into, each other's cultures, yet all too often little or no effort is made to do so. Historical factors are partly to blame for this, such as the 'we're better than them' attitudes which still exist as a hangover from the colonial era. But there is no room for this today. Failure to respect the customs, values and traditions of other countries and peoples is a recipe for disaster in a multicultural, inter-dependent world.

Silent language

The anthropologist, Edward Hall, coined the phrase 'the silent language' to describe out-of-awareness aspects of communication. People of western European descent, he argued, live in a 'word world' and often fail to realize the significance of the 'language of behaviour'. If we don't at least try to understand this language, we can only blame ourselves when things go wrong. He gives instances in which inappropriate non-verbal behaviour, coupled with general cultural insensitivity, can cause poor communication, or even cause it to break down altogether. Take the case in which negotiations between American and Greek officials had reached stalemate. Examination revealed that the American habit of being outspoken and forthright was regarded by the Greeks as indicating a lack of finesse, which made them reluctant to negotiate. When the Americans wanted to limit the length of meetings and to reach agreement on general principles first, leaving the details to be sorted out by sub-committees, the Greeks saw this as a device to pull the wool over their eyes. The basic difference between the two negotiating styles was that the Greeks preferred to work out the details in front of all concerned – regardless of how long it took.

In another case, an American attaché, new to a Latin country, tried to arrange a meeting with his ministerial opposite number. All kinds of messages came back that the time was not yet ripe for such a meeting. The American persisted and was eventually granted an appointment. When he arrived, he was asked to wait in an outer office. The time of the appointment came and went. After 15 minutes, he asked the minister's secretary to make sure the minister knew he was waiting. Time passed. Twenty minutes, 30 minutes, 45 minutes. At this point, he jumped up and told the secretary he had been 'cooling his heels' long enough and that he was 'sick and tired' of this kind of treatment. What he had failed to grasp is that a 45-minute waiting time in that country was equivalent to a five-minute waiting time in America.

Effective cross-cultural communication is so important in the modern world that breakdowns like these need to be studied for the lessons they can teach us. They also make it increasingly important that people who live and work in countries other than their own should be given training so that they recognize differences in local body language as well as the local spoken language. While quite a lot of research has been carried out on differences in the way various peoples around the world use body language, it has tended to focus on the Americans, the Japanese, the Arabs and some European countries. More needs to be done to include people from other cultures given the far greater mobility afforded by open borders and cheaper travel today.

Eye signals

In research into the use of eye contact, for instance, it has been observed that Greeks look at each other more in public places, whether in direct communication or just observation. In fact, they feel quite upset if other people do not show an equal curiosity in them and feel they are being ignored. On the other hand, Swedes have been found to look at each other less often than other Europeans, but they look for longer.

Arabs are very dependent on eye contact when conversing. They look at each other when listening and when talking, however they interact less successfully with someone whose eyes cannot be seen. The Japanese look at other people very little and tend to focus their eyes on the other person's neck when conversing. Americans and British, on the other hand, tend to be relatively restrained in their facial expressions, while Italians tend to be much more expressive. The Japanese keep a straight face in public and make more use of smiles when greeting others, particularly in business and formal meetings.

Figure 1.1 Eye contact.

Thoughts and actions

We communicate using gestures and body posture far more than we realize. Gesticulations, facial expressions, head movements, in fact all kinds of actions involving the face, hands and body, take the place of words on many occasions. It's as if we are dancing to the tune of our thoughts, investing what we say with additional meaning and weight. Sometimes thoughts and feelings make themselves known without us intending them to do so – what we mean by *betraying our thoughts*.

In many cases actions speak louder than words. How a person stands can indicate how they are feeling about something. We call someone 'uptight' when they seem taut and controlling, and 'defensive' when they cross their arms and hunch their backs. The Japanese bow when greeting and saying farewells, with persons of lower status bowing lower than those of high status. Germans on the other hand maintain a more upright posture than people from Latin countries. Italians and Arabs stand closer to other people when conversing, whereas Germans stand further apart.

The Japanese use formal gestures to summon others to them, such as extending the arm with palm downwards and fluttering the fingers. To suggest that someone is a liar, they lick a forefinger and stroke an eyebrow. The British are more likely to nod and look downwards, saying nothing, yet signifying their doubt.

In the USA, you can signal that everything is OK by forming a circle with the thumb and index finger and spreading out the rest of the fingers, but in Japan the same gesture means money, in France it means 'zero', in Scandinavia and parts of central Europe it is regarded as vulgar, and in some south American countries it has obscene connotations.

In Hindu and Muslim cultures it is customary to use the right hand when preparing and eating food because the left hand is considered unclean due to its use in bodily hygiene. Equally, pointing the soles of your feet towards another person is considered offensive – something that globe-trotting backpackers should note.

Westerners tend to think that a smile always reflects warmth or happiness, yet in some parts of Asia it can also indicate displeasure since overt expression of negative feelings is discouraged. Silence is similarly misinterpreted. Whereas the Japanese are comfortable with silences, particularly during negotiations, Americans and British often find them unnerving. We shall return to this subject in more detail in Chapter 8.

Touch and tone

Latins touch each other more readily in everyday social situations than northern Europeans, while Arab men will frequently hold hands while walking and talking – something which Europeans often misinterpret. The Japanese touch each other very little in public, though they have a tradition of bathing together without any connotation of immodesty. Western women kiss, hug and touch each other socially, while it is frowned upon for Arab women to be touched at all in public.

We often pat children on the head as a sign of affection, but in Muslim countries the head is regarded as the seat of mental and spiritual powers. Accordingly, it should not be touched. In the West we scratch our heads when we are puzzled, while in Japan, the same action is interpreted as showing anger.

Amongst other non-verbal forms of communication tone of voice is particularly important across cultures. Emotions can be gauged from how people speak even if the spoken language is not properly understood. But a word of warning here: Latin languages are often spoken with far greater emphasis than, say, English, and are accompanied by similarly expressive hand and arm movements. To the more reserved northern European this can sound like shouting, or even criticism, when it is simply uninhibited conversation. In other words, it is up to you, the listener, to recognize and appreciate cultural differences in the way we communicate, not to over-react to types of behaviour with which we are unfamiliar. Just because something does not conform to our own notions of acceptability, doesn't mean that it is wrong.

PERSONAL SPACE

Americans generally prefer more personal space than people in Mediterranean and Latin American cultures, and more than men in Muslim cultures. This is because space is associated with independence and individual rights to privacy. In a recent study, a Brazilian man working as a waiter in an American restaurant found that his habit of casually touching his colleagues when talking resulted in him being rejected. Confused as to why this was happening, he started to observe how Americans interact and eventually realized that they dislike being touched by people they don't know.

In another case, an American student, who was reading philosophy at the Sorbonne in Paris, was surprised to find that his Algerian neighbour had a habit of standing and talking barely inches from his face. Not wanting to seem rude by backing away, the student admitted that such close proximity made him extremely uncomfortable. If an American was to get that close, he said, he would have reacted quite differently.

What this tells us is that different cultures have different 'rules of engagement' and that breaking them, even without knowing, can have negative results. Having said this, it is rare for people to have confrontations over personal space, probably because it's hard to tell someone from another culture to back off without appearing offensive. Much more likely is that we will angle our bodies in such a way as to create a buffer zone between them and us. Essentially there is no difference between us and the rest of the animal kingdom in this respect. Animals don't take kindly to being touched by strangers, so why should we? (See Chapter 10 for more.)

Universal body language

So what does all this tell us? Essentially, it is that while we may be very different from each other, there are nevertheless universally understood examples of body language which bind us together. For example, Ekman and Friesen found that people of 13 different cultures were able to distinguish accurately between the non-verbal expressions of joy, surprise, fear, anger, sadness and disgust, while Michael Argyle identified seven elements which commonly occur in greetings:

- *close proximity and face-to-face orientation*
- *the eyebrow flash (raised up on greeting)*
- *smiling*
- *direct eye contact*
- *bodily contact, even in most otherwise non-contact cultures*
- *presenting of the palm of the hand, either to shake or simply to be seen*
- *upward head toss or nod in the form of a bow.*

Though it is generally the case that people smile when they are happy and scowl when they are angry, there are lots of ways in which we show non-verbal dissatisfaction with another's behaviour – the shrug, for example. To minimize the risk of causing offence, or of being offended, it is important to use those aspects of body language that have universal currency as much as possible. Smiles, eyebrow flashes, cocking the head, presenting the palm of the right hand in greeting – all help to ease you through the initial phases of encounters, enabling you then to use other descriptive gestures to indicate what you want to say or do.

Generally speaking, a friendly expression and an indication of interest in the other person will help to smooth over awkwardness and embarrassment. If this is supported by some attempt to learn key words and phrases from the spoken language, communication is immediately enhanced. This way, your opposite number will almost certainly meet you half way. Even those who live in quite formal cultures, like the Japanese, respond very favourably when appropriate body language is accompanied by a few carefully chosen words.

Business body language

There are pitfalls to be avoided when conducting business in other countries, particularly in our use and understanding of body language differences. As we have seen, awareness of the passage of time varies across cultures. In the USA, the obsession with time and scheduling means that punctuality and efficiency are expected, and competitiveness encouraged. Americans prefer a brisk, businesslike approach and are gregarious at first meeting. Differences in status are minimized.

By comparison, in Arab countries, persons of senior rank and status tend to be recognized first. Arabs like expressiveness and periodic displays of emotion. Group-style business meetings with several things happening at once are typical. It is not unusual for participants to enter into close, personal discussion whatever other conversation is going on around them.

Africans like to get to know someone before getting down to business and the general chat at the beginning of business meetings can seem like time-wasting to foreigners. Time is flexible and people who appear to be in a hurry are mistrusted. Lateness is a normal part of life. Respect is expected to be shown to older people.

In China, people do not like to be singled out as unique and prefer to be treated as part of a team. Women often occupy important posts and expect to be treated as equals. Long-standing relationships are respected and are worth taking time to establish. Even in the age of email, personal contact is highly valued. Several negotiating sessions will normally be required, as the Chinese do not like to rush things.

Robert Moran graphically illustrates how things can so easily go wrong when you fail to observe local cultural differences in body language. For example, if you wish to catch the attention of a waiter at a business lunch in Western countries a common way is to hold a hand up with the index finger extended. In Asia, however, this is the way you would call a dog or some other animal. In Arab countries, showing the soles of your feet is an insult. An Arab may also insult someone by holding their hand in front of the person's face.

Figure 1.2 Finger signals – European.

Figure 1.3 Finger signals – Asian.

Figure 1.4 This would be an insult to an Arab.

In most parts of the world, shaking the head means 'No', but in Arab countries and in parts of Greece, Yugoslavia, Bulgaria and Turkey, a more usual way is to toss the head to one side, perhaps clicking the tongue as well. In Japan, a person may move his right hand backwards and forwards to communicate a refusal or disagreement. In Africa agreement is shown by holding an open palm upright and smacking it with a closed fist. Arabs will show agreement by extending clasped hands with the index fingers pointing towards the other person.

Clearly, anyone who undertakes international business should do a little research beforehand in order to find out what body language pitfalls need to be avoided. It may make the difference between success and failure. In a highly competitive world, the businessperson who fails to appreciate the power of body language can end up paying a high price.

You can improve your knowledge of body language as you go along by recording your responses electronically, or in a notebook. This way, you will have something to refer to when you read through the review section following each exercise.

Exercise 1: Multicultural body language

Select five people from different cultures and observe how their body language differs. How do they greet each other, or say farewell? How close do they stand or sit? Are there variations in facial, hand and body movements and postures? Do they observe silences more or less than each other? In particular, note the role of women in the company of men from different parts of the world.

Make notes (discreetly) about clothing styles, including colours, formality of dress, patterns, and the extent of covering-up.

(Contd)

Record as much detail as you can about eye contact patterns, facial expressions, gestures, proximity and bodily contact.

When you have collected as much information as you reasonably can, analyse it. What seem to be the main differences between them? What are the similarities? What differences are there between the sexes? What are your thoughts on these?

EXERCISE REVIEW

It is quite possible that you will have collected a rich amount of data which will repay careful analysis and tell you many things about how people of different races and cultures interact. For example:

▶ *Differences in the way ethnic and cultural groups greet and touch each other. White Caucasians tend to touch each other less than southern Europeans. Afro-Caribbeans often touch each other on the arms and shoulders during conversation.*
▶ *The Chinese and Japanese observe greater formality than people of other races, though they maintain greater eye contact during encounters.*
▶ *The facial expressions and hand gestures of most white people are more restrained than those of Afro-Caribbeans, but less so than the Chinese and Japanese.*
▶ *Muslim women will often cover their faces and bodies when in public.*
▶ *People (particularly women) from the Indian sub-continent and from Africa choose more vivid colours and stronger patterns for their clothing than Westerners.*
▶ *Attitudes to children and children's behaviour differ markedly across cultures.*

Further exercises and experiments

Foreign films
Watch one or two foreign films, preferably where you do not understand the language. Note instances of body language that are unusual, together with what they mean (if in doubt, try to consult a native of the country for an explanation). Look particularly at the use of eye contact, head nods, gesture, posture, and so on. Listen for tone of voice, speech errors, speed of speaking, pitch and so forth. Try to watch films from, say, France, Germany, Russia, India, and the Far East to get a good coverage of different cultures.

Business body language
Observe business people talking in a public place, such as a hotel lobby or airport lounge. What are their most frequently used non-verbal behaviours? Do they differ in any way from members of the general public? Consider appearance and physique, timing and synchronization, and proximity and orientation as well as other aspects of body language.

I'm a stranger here myself
With a group of friends who are willing to participate in the exercise, act as if you were a foreigner who does not speak the language. How do others react to you? What are the most useful forms of body language? Are there any situations you find impossible to deal with?

2

Everyday encounters

In this chapter you will learn:
• *the role of body language in everyday life situations*
• *how to gauge the meaning of body language signals.*

Unless you are a hermit, encountering people is a regular occurrence, though the interaction you have with them can range from the briefest acknowledgement in the street to complex social situations requiring a multitude of different responses. In each of these encounters our body language continuously supports, contradicts, regulates or controls what is taking place. It forms a constant stream of activity that informs us about the 'state of play' between ourselves and others and often determines the success or failure of these interactions.

First impressions

In the first few minutes of an encounter, particularly one with a stranger, we are heavily dependent upon body language for 'sizing up' the other person; what he or she is like, how easy or difficult they are going to be to deal with and whether we are going to like them. We depend on non-verbal clues because the opening stages of conversations tend to centre on small talk and general trivia, like the weather, and we do not begin to get detailed verbal information until later. Generally we defer our judgements until we have this information.

First impressions tend to last. The fact that they are formed very quickly does not seem to detract from their strength and permanence. Indeed, they can even be influenced by what we are told in advance of meeting someone. If we're told we will like that person because they are friendly, this affects how we respond when we do meet them. More often than not we rate someone's attractiveness and presence before anything else. General appearance counts for a lot, even before race, age and nationality are taken into account. Once we have these first impressions we begin to form initial judgements as to educational and cultural background, occupation, social and political attitudes and so forth. Our responses to people older than ourselves will differ from those we make to younger people. Similarly, we respond differently to the status of the person we are dealing with, though traditional distinctions based on class and social position are less common as society becomes increasingly achievement-oriented.

Breaking the ice

At the start of an encounter there is usually a great deal of eye contact as we open channels of communication with the other person. Facial expressions tend to be positive and if we already know them the chances are that we will greet them with a handshake, a hug or maybe hold the upper arm with the free hand while shaking their hand. Raised eyebrows (the eyebrow 'flash') indicate initial recognition, followed by a cocking back of the head as we receive the news they have for us. Standing in close proximity and leaning towards the other person indicate growing rapport.

These preliminaries are usually followed by stereotypical exchanges of the 'How are you?' 'I'm fine, how are you?' variety. At this point, the conversation will either move on to more substantial matters, or conclude naturally. If it continues, body language tends to settle down with facial expressions and head movements altering to reflect what is being said. Posture relaxes and gestures emphasize the points being made. Within a very short space of time you will be unconsciously harmonizing, or *synchronizing*, with your opposite number. (See Chapters 8 and 9.)

During investigations of non-verbal communication in encounters, Mark Knapp and his colleagues identified a number of body language behaviours that indicate when conversations are coming to an end. Referred to as 'the rhetoric of goodbye' these include breaking eye contact, pointing the body in the direction one intends to leave, increased head and leg movements and smiling. If seated, uncrossing the legs and striking a foot against the floor while using the hands to lever oneself out of the chair, makes clear the intention to go.

Small talk

Vague, inconsequential chats about nothing in particular may seem hardly worth spending time on, yet they can be more important than you think. During small talk, what is being said is often less significant than what is being conveyed in body language terms. Next time you encounter someone for a casual chat, or meet a stranger at a party, try noting his or her body language and consider how it is being used, for example:

▶ **Eye contact** *Do they appear to want more or less of it? How dilated are their pupils? Do they keep looking around at other people, or is their full attention given to you?*
▶ **Facial expressions** *Are they positive or negative? Are there smiles and signs of interest, or scowls of disgust? Are there few or many changes in expression? Can you spot momentary changes in expression?*
▶ **Head movements** *Do they show interest by cocking their heads? Do they encourage you to speak with head nods? Do they respond to your head nods? Does the rhythm of their head movements fit the rhythm of their speech?*
▶ **Gestures** *Few or many? Are they expressive? Are they appropriate? Are they open or closed? Are the arms folded*

in front of themselves? If they cross their legs, which way do they cross them, towards you or away from you?

▶ **Posture** *Is it upright or stooping? Which way is the individual leaning?*

▶ **Proximity and orientation** *Do they approach closely or not? If you move closer, do they back away or turn away from you? Is their orientation direct or indirect? Is it symmetrical or asymmetrical? Horizontal or vertical?*

▶ **Bodily contact** *Do they use any? In greetings only? Are they touchers or non-touchers? Which parts of the body do they touch most frequently as they are talking? Arms, hands, shoulders, backs or elsewhere? Are you comfortable with it?*

Next, assess their appearance and physique and how you feel it affects your response to them. Do you find them attractive? Are they taller than you or shorter? Do you like their body shape? Does it matter to you? Then ask yourself if you are *synchronizing* – meaning that the discussion you are having dovetails neatly together – or do you find yourselves both speaking at the same time. If so, why? On the other hand, is the failure to synchronize due to nervousness or some other factor? Finally, listen to the non-verbal aspects of their speech. Do they make many errors? How fast do they talk? Loud or soft? Harsh or smooth in tone? How do you respond?

There are, of course, many other questions that can be posed, but these should provide you with a simple, yet systematic method of evaluating how other people use body language in everyday encounters. Don't worry if you can't find answers to all of them at this stage. We will be dealing with them in greater detail in Part two.

Body lies

The one thing none of us really wants is to find out that someone is deceiving us, because it implies that they aren't what they *appear* to be. Most people don't set out to deceive others, but we're all guilty of it sometimes. We like to call minor deceptions 'white lies' and to *appear* honest – even if we aren't being totally honest with ourselves. But appearances can be deceptive. US Presidents Richard Nixon and Bill Clinton both faced impeachment because they tried to cover up the truth. As in everyday life, deception gets found out. 'In law and in journalism, in government and in the social sciences', wrote the American philosopher Sissela Bok, 'deception is taken for granted when it is felt to be excusable by those who tell lies and who tend also to make the rules.'

So, in real life, being deceived is an everyday hazard and we need to be on the look-out for it. Certain kinds of body language occur more often when people are lying than when they are telling the truth. For example, what is called *leakage* refers to non-verbal behaviour which an individual fails to control, such as shuffling the feet, twitching the toes, crossing and uncrossing the legs. Facial expressions may be capable of control, and an accomplished liar may be able to maintain eye contact with his listener, but the movements of the hands are less easily controllable. One gesture commonly associated with deception is the **hand shrug** in which the hands are rotated so as to expose the palms. It is as if deceivers try to enlist our sympathy to cover the deception – 'what, me?'

Figure 2.1 Sign of deception – hand shrug.

Figure 2.2 Sign of deception – touching the side of the nose.

Touching the side of the nose, touching the eye, licking the lips, drumming the fingers and gripping arm rests, occur more often when people are attempting to deceive others. Blushing, perspiration, voice tremors, gulping, shaking and playing with pencils or spectacles are other commonly observed behaviours. This suggests that *stress* has its own distinctive body language. As Sigmund Freud wrote: 'He that has eyes to see and ears to hear may convince himself that no mortal can keep a secret. If his lips are silent, he chatters with his fingertips. Betrayal oozes out of every pore.'

Liars are less likely to engage in bodily contact or even to approach closely. Their body language very often contradicts their spoken words. For instance, they may say they would be very willing to submit themselves to a full enquiry and yet their facial expression, posture and gestures will suggest otherwise. When Albert Mehrabian investigated how people behaved when they were conveying truthful messages as against those that were not, he discovered that those who were lying talked less, talked more slowly, and made more errors of speech. Additionally, their rate of body movement also seemed to be slower. What this tells us is that body language can be just as good a guide to the truth as the most eloquently spoken words.

Exercise 2: Age and sex

Record the voices of several people of various ages, with males and females in roughly equal proportions. Have them talk about subjects that will not give their age away (e.g. avoid having an older man talking about his war stories). Play the voices back and see if they can identify the age and sex of the speakers from voice alone.

If you are unable to enlist the participation of other people, sit with your back to the television and see if you can guess the age and sex of several speakers. Make a note of your conclusions then watch the picture as well as listening to the sound and see if this helps you to decide how accurate you were. If you're not sure how old the TV personalities are, check them out on the internet.

EXERCISE REVIEW

As you might expect, it is not too difficult, in most cases, to identify a person's gender from voice alone. It is often also quite easy to identify race or nationality. You will probably have found that children's voices can be spotted without difficulty. Elderly people often have a voice quality that is relatively easy to distinguish. The real problem comes with those whose ages range between 30 and 70.

However, there are some clues which may help here. Volume tends to be higher with younger people than with older ones. Tone tends to deepen with age, though it often becomes sharper and more fragile-sounding with extreme age, perhaps even with a tremor. Younger voices have a more confident, even brash, sound to them in many cases. Allowing five years either side for age predictions, if you correctly allocated more than two-thirds of the voices you have done well. (See Chapter 14 for more.)

Further exercises and experiments

Who said that?
Obtain photographs of several people, taken in what for them is a normal environment. Then get them to tape record a couple of minutes' speech about a topic that will not give the environment away. See if other people can match the voices to the photographs. How successful are they?

How many people do you meet a day?
Make a list of all the people you meet in a day. Be careful not to miss anyone out. Then classify them into friends, family, acquaintances, strangers and 'others' (people like waiters, bus drivers, canteen staff, and so on with whom the interaction is purely functional). What is the pattern of your daily interactions? Are you spending as much time with friends and family as you would like? If not, is there anything you can do about it?

What's the first thing you notice?
When you meet strangers, what is the first thing you notice about them? Does it differ for males and females? For older people and for younger people? What are the physical characteristics you look for (or respond to) in an attractive stranger of the opposite sex?

Tell the truth
Watch a television programme in which people claim to be telling the truth, or get a group together to play a truth game, and see how accurately you can identify the truth tellers from the deceivers. What deception cues help you to eliminate those least likely to be truthful? Ask those who seem to be able to pick out the right person more often than other people if they know how they do it. You will probably find that many of them put it down to a hunch and are totally unaware of how they have been influenced by body language.

3

Personal attraction

In this chapter you will learn:
- *about the part played by body language in relationships*
- *how non-verbal behaviour can be used to make you more attractive.*

In the 1987 Oscar-nominated thriller *Fatal Attraction*, scheming Alex Forrest (Glenn Close) tells infatuated family-man Dan Gallagher (Michael Douglas) 'We were attracted to each other at the party, that was obvious! You're on your own for the night, that's also obvious... we're two adults...' If you don't know the ending, try watching the film, and while you are doing it, ask yourself what it is that is so fatally attractive about dangerous liaisons.

The problem with the notion of 'attraction' is that it confuses physical attributes and sexual response with characteristics of personality, individual skills and interests. Several studies have shown that being talented, warm and responsive, kind, sensitive, interesting, poised, sociable and outgoing, are considered attractive. By comparison with 'unattractive people', those who have these qualities are seen as being more intelligent and as having a more socially desirable personality, higher occupational status, and better prospects in the marriage stakes.

But if it's not purely someone's physical attributes that makes you find them attractive, what it is that turns you on to them?

We know that virtually all communication is non-verbal, so it must be body language that ticks the boxes. For example, is it the sound of their voice (rather than what they are saying), the eye contact and dilation of their pupils as they respond to you, or even the way they move that attracts you to them?

Studies over the years have shown that men look for those characteristics in women that clearly differentiate them from men: fuller lips, narrower eyebrows, a softer complexion, absence of facial hair, firm breasts, a narrower waist, relatively broad hips and long legs. When asked to rate photographs of attractive females, most male respondents pick stereotypically 'sexy' woman, even if their own partners do not match the stereotype.

It is not as easy to identify what it is that women find attractive in men. While some might go for the classic 'hunter-gatherer' stereotype who oozes masculinity and affords protection, there is plenty of anecdotal evidence drawn from magazines that women are more interested in a man's eyes, whether he has a sense of humour and is dependable, and then whether he's slim and has well-rounded, sexy buttocks. It's mainly men who think women look for tall, muscular, well-endowed superhunks.

In reality, personal attraction doesn't depend simply on appearance and physique. The 'ideal' face or body is exactly that – an ideal. In truth, most of us have less-than-perfect faces and figures, but that doesn't mean we are less attractive. Cook and McHenry quote a study which suggests that the ideal face for both sexes is oval in shape, with a clear complexion, large eyes, a straight nose, a medium-sized mouth, ears that do not protrude, long eyelashes, bushy eyebrows for men and fine eyebrows for women. And yet no face is perfectly symmetrical, so variations from the ideal are inevitable.

The truth is that there are no hard and fast rules about attraction. As the old adage *beauty is in the eye of the beholder* suggests, attraction has less to do with the object of our interest than how we respond to it. When you think about it, a beautiful painting in one person's opinion may be quite ordinary to another. A gorgeous hunk to one woman may be just a nice-looking guy to another. Personal taste, then, plays an important role in determining whom we find attractive and what we find attractive about them.

Boy meets girl

Imagine this situation: a young guy enters a club, pauses inside the door to look around and wanders over towards the bar. He grabs the last barstool, slides onto it and raises a finger to the barman to indicate that he'd like a drink. While he waits, his eyes fix on a pretty girl reflected in the mirrors in front of him. She appears to be talking animatedly to a girlfriend. Every so often she flashes a look in his direction via the mirrors. He catches one of these glances and, for a second, their eyes lock before she looks away.

What happens next? Does he hold her gaze and smile when she next looks up? Let's say he does. But what kind of smile? A warm, friendly, 'hi', or a 'here I am, you'll be making a big mistake if you ignore me' kind of smile?

A friend of his rolls up and slaps him on the back and they laugh together about something. The girl looks up and observes them in turn. She mentions something to her friend and they both look up. Our guy notices them looking and winks in the mirror. They giggle and ostentatiously wink back. What does that mean? Has he blown it? Do they think he's just another arrogant jerk, or is this a little bit of teasing to see what he's made of? Who knows. It's early yet and there's no point in rushing.

Time passes. The girls ask the barman to hold their seats while they go to the ladies' room. As they walk past the boys, they raise their eyes. 'Fancy a drink?' our guy asks, scanning their faces for a positive reaction. The girls nod without turning, their swaying hips indicating that the first major hurdle in the encounter has been successfully surmounted – the invitation to interact.

Cut to the dance floor half an hour later. The music's too loud to talk so communication takes place through their body language. Heightened senses quickly log personal information: tall, slim, shapely, nice touch, no body odour... Without knowing it they are sizing each other up, double-checking reality against first impressions. They dance closer together. The other two wander off. He likes her smile, she likes his eyes. He's paying her attention, not surveying the competition. She dances ever closer to him, raising her hair with her hands and leaning forward to expose her cleavage. He can't take his eyes off her.

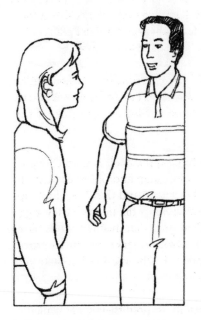 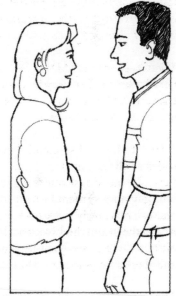

Figure 3.1 Boy meets girl: You're nice – eye contact.   *Figure 3.2 I like you – close proximity.*

Figure 3.3 Interested? – head back, hands in hair.

Figure 3.4 No thanks – self-wrap, legs crossed, eyes away.

Good mates

In situations like these, actions undoubtedly speak louder than words. In the animal kingdom – and we are part of it – body language has always been used to select the perfect mate. It doesn't matter whether we are just being friendly, or actively looking for a partner, the same non-verbal techniques of communication apply:

▶ **Eye contact** *is important whether we are just good friends in animated conversation, or lovers sharing unspoken emotions. Generally speaking though, you don't gaze into a friend's or colleague's eyes during an everyday encounter. So the duration of a gaze indicates increased interest in the other person.*

- **Facial expressions** *tend to be more positive when you are in the presence of someone who matters to you. After all, a smile is indicative of something pleasing, whereas a scowl is the opposite.*
- **Relaxed postures and gestures** *are more welcoming and suggest a lack of self-consciousness.*
- **Close proximity and direct body orientation** *indicate liking, and wanting to get to know someone.*
- **Timing and synchronization** *become naturally attuned the more you warm towards each other.*
- **Bodily contact** *becomes more frequent and extensive the closer you are.*

Winning ways

Paying attention to these key areas of body language can make the difference between hitting it off with someone and losing the chance to find out more. But there are five additional factors that contribute to the success of encounters – **rapport, empathy, synergy, self-disclosure** and **charisma.**

RAPPORT

Successful communication depends upon the establishment of rapport with others. To do this you need to recognize what you have in common and to work towards cementing bonds that can be relied upon in the future. This involves:

- *treating the other person as an equal*
- *maintaining a warm, friendly manner*
- *finding common interests and experiences*
- *displaying a sympathetic interest*
- *giving your full attention*
- *providing time for things to develop*
- *listening carefully to what others say*

- ▶ *reducing anxiety or defensiveness on their part*
- ▶ *echoing, not mimicking, their body language.*

To be a good communicator you need to be able to establish rapport without making it look as if you are trying too hard. It's about making the other person feel comfortable with you. Very often, the more you warm towards each other, the more your body language synchronizes – as if you are subconsciously mirroring each other's actions. Observations of the way in which we succeed or fail in creating rapport have led to the development of modelling techniques which focus upon actions and behaviours that positively or negatively influence the outcome of personal encounters. (See neurolinguistic programming (NLP) in Chapter 5.)

EMPATHY

Empathy is a term often used to describe the ability to experience a situation or problem from someone else's point of view. Being able to read someone successfully is a first step towards getting on with them. In counselling, for example, having an empathic relationship with the client means being sensitive to his or her feelings and being able to adjust one's responses to suit the situation in hand. Being aware of negative body language can provide useful clues to the state of mind of the individual.

In personal relationships you may have to break the ice or ease tension in order to get on. To get closer, note the other person's body language and synchronize with it. This often makes them feel more comfortable and enables them to relax. But don't *mimic* their behaviour. This will just make you appear false. Empathy is the art of relating to someone by watching and listening without judging.

SYNERGY

Sometimes things go so well that you don't need any extra encouragement to make an encounter work. This is called synergy, and it often happens when the occasion acquires a dimension of magic – when it seems that nothing can go wrong. It's as if an extra dimension is being added – and most of it is conveyed through body language. Synergy is said to occur when the outcome of a situation is greater than the sum of the inputs. It is sometimes described by the formula 2 + 2 = 5. An example of non-verbal synergy is when you meet someone with whom you just 'click' – you don't have to say anything to know that you're getting on well together. Your body language is doing that for you.

SELF-DISCLOSURE

If you are shy or reticent about letting people know too much about you, it's not always easy to open up to others, but if you don't give, you don't get. What you do is as important as what you say, so self-disclosure is essential to how you convey a positive impression of who you are. Sidney Jourard coined the term 'the transparent self' to describe the willingness of people to disclose information about themselves to others. He found that they disclose more, and behave differently, when the person with whom they are interacting is also prepared to disclose something about themselves. Therefore, being prepared to volunteer information verbally or non-verbally is mutually beneficial.

CHARISMA

Stars are said to possess charisma – that extra quality which makes them stand out from the crowd, or draws others to them like magnets. But what is this mysterious quality – and is it something we can 'bottle' to make us more attractive to others? Social psychologists have long wanted the answer to these questions and it is even thought that the quality resides in the minds of the fans, not the stars. In other words, *we* make them stars through our adoration of them. Certainly body language has to play an important part in all of this. We talk about charismatic people being *head and shoulders* above the rest, even *having us in the palm of their hands*. But whatever the reasons there's little doubt that charisma is a quality that some have which makes others defer to them, causing them to be raised on a pedestal in our eyes.

Actually, charisma is present to some degree in lots of people – the guy at work who's 'a bit of a character'; the captain of the local rugby team who so-and-so's got a crush on; the train guard who chats happily to her passengers over the public address system. More often than not these people display dominant rather than submissive body language and seem to blossom in the limelight of others' attention.

Celebrities love to be looked at – perhaps that's why we call it stargazing – but equally they do a lot of gazing themselves. In fact eye contact is one of the most significant aspects of the star's body language. They use what is called **anticipatory scanning** when moving through an audience, picking out and focusing on certain people, whether they are aware of doing so or not. They smile a lot and use constantly changing facial expressions – though some recording artists prefer the sullen, moody look, which, curiously, can be equally engaging.

A common head movement with celebrities is to tilt, or toss the head backwards as if awaiting applause. **Open gestures** signify their confidence and assurance of receiving the 'embrace' of the audience. Their arms reach out and their hands are raised palm-up as if to draw the audience to them. Some gestures are deliberately seductive – running their hands over their bodies, stroking their hair, picking pieces of fluff off clothing, reaching out to touch people in the front row. But this is what the audience often wants – to be seduced, to fall in love, to offer oneself in submission to our idols. That's what animal attraction is all about.

Exercise 3: Peoplewatching

Have you ever sat in a café, on a beach, or on a park bench just peoplewatching? If you have, you may have found yourself scoring passers-by on a scale of one to ten for attractiveness, dullness, body size, clothes and so on. It might not be very accurate, or fair, for that matter, but it's one of the ways we make our minds up about people we don't know.

Using the rating scale in Figure 3.5, rate several strangers over the next week. If you can, enlist the participation of others so that you finish up with a reasonably large number of completed scales.

EXERCISE REVIEW

Two things should emerge from this exercise. You should obtain a clearer idea of precisely which non-verbal behaviours and physical characteristics appeal to you in other people. You should also find that your ratings tend to agree with those of others who took part in the experiment (if you were fortunate enough to find some friends or colleagues who would).

Which is more important, appearance or some other aspect of body language?

Score people 1 to 10 on each of the following aspects of appearance and other uses of body language. Place an X in the appropriate box.

	1	2	3	4	5	6	7	8	9	10
Hair										
Forehead										
Shape of head										
Face										
Eyes										
Nose										
Mouth										
Ears										
Neck										
Skin										
Body build										
Shoulders										
Chest/breasts										
Arms										

(Contd)

	1	2	3	4	5	6	7	8	9	10
Hands										
Waist										
Buttocks										
Abdomen and pelvis										
Thighs										
Knees										
Calves										
Feet										
Shape of legs										
Length of legs										
Eye contact										
Facial expression										
Head movements										
Gestures										
Posture										
Use of personal space										
Bodily contact										
Timing and awareness										
Non-verbal signals										
TOTALS:										
(For a o rating simply leave blank) Max = 330										

Figure 3.5 Personal attraction assessment scale.

Further exercises and experiments

Who makes the first move?
Observe people in a place where they are meeting for the first time (e.g. a party or a wine bar). Who initiates interaction? The man or the woman? Who makes eye contact first and who holds that gaze? What kinds of body language bring them together? Do same-sex encounters differ from mixed-sex encounters?

Sex appeal
What are the body language components of sex appeal? Try to list them using the behaviours referred to in this chapter. If you

can, compare your assessment with those of other people. Do your impressions agree? If not, why not?

Partners for life
Study the body language of people you know who have been happily married for at least ten years. Do they echo each other's postures and gestures? Do they echo any other aspects of body language? How does their behaviour differ when they are apart from when they are together?

4

....

Body language at work

In this chapter you will learn:
- *about the role of body language in the working environment*
- *what being a success really requires*
- *presentation skills and why they count*
- *why body language matters in face-to-face occupations*.

Being a success at work involves a whole range of skills, some of which you may not even be aware you have. Body language is particularly important in occupations requiring face-to-face communication with members of the public. Whether you are a nurse, teacher, receptionist, salesperson, business executive, television personality or pop star, being able to put people at ease involves non-verbal skills that maximize attention and foster rapport. But what happens if you aren't very good at doing this? Do your promotion prospects suffer? Do people treat you differently from the fast-trackers? The fact is that many talented people fail to get noticed, and lose out in the promotion stakes because they think that success is based on what they do, rather than on what they're seen to do. Impressions count. If you are a quiet little mouse you are less likely to be noticed than the outward-going, charismatic members of the team.

Self-presentation

There are four basic styles of self-presentation which distinguish the wallflowers from the wolves – **submissive**, **assertive**, **manipulative** and **aggressive**.

SUBMISSIVE

Some people are naturally quiet because of the way they have been brought up. They often lack confidence because they simply haven't been made to feel good about themselves. If you aren't encouraged by the people that matter – your parents, teachers, and work colleagues – you are unlikely to shine in the company of those who have. Not being told that you are good at things, or that people are proud of you, can make you defensive, self-conscious, apologetic, self-deprecating and submissive in adult life. By carrying these characteristics into the workplace you are judged not only on performance, but also on self-presentation, much of which will be negative. This is where derogatory terms like 'wimp', 'crawler', 'creep' and 'loser' come from – as if you somehow 'lower yourself' in the eyes of others. The kinds of body language that betray feelings of inadequacy include:

▶ *quietness*
▶ *nervous disposition*
▶ *slumped posture*
▶ *poor eye contact*
▶ *fidgeting*
▶ *faltering voice*
▶ *face and body wrapping*
▶ *trying too hard.*

ASSERTIVE

By comparison, assertive body language conveys confidence and, rightly or wrongly, gives the impression of experience and authority. If you seem on top of things others will assume that you are, and accord you respect. Assertiveness might make you appear 'pushy', but if you use relaxed body language you come across as self-assured and sympathetic. Many of the best managers are those described as 'firm, but fair' and whose body language includes:

▶ *an upright, relaxed body posture*
▶ *direct eye contact*
▶ *open gestures*
▶ *relaxed facial expressions*
▶ *unambiguous hand signals*
▶ *a clear, confident voice.*

MANIPULATIVE

Manipulators tend to get their own way because they are clever. They calculate and use situations to their advantage. While this could describe many people in business, it only has a negative ring to it when it involves insincerity. If you are patronizing, two-faced, over-friendly and tend to make ends justify means, you are probably insincere and not to be trusted. People who display these kinds of characteristics often have a body language which includes:

▶ *exaggerated gestures and eye contact*
▶ *a sugary tone of voice*
▶ *an overly laid-back posture*
▶ *a patronizing habit of touching and patting.*

AGGRESSIVE

You can always tell an aggressive person at work. They are the ones who shout and use sarcasm, criticism, blame and putting people down as a way of maintaining control. Ironically, aggressive people are often the ones lacking self-confidence and use these negative weapons as a defence against being found out. Effective managers are successful because they are self-assured, not because they hold power. It's all about being comfortable

with yourself. If you rant and rave all the time it suggests that you are uncomfortable, if not out of control. Leadership qualities are those which inspire trust – not fear – in others, which is why good teamwork depends on mutual trust and understanding. Aggression has its tell-tale body language signatures:

- ▶ *a confrontational posture*
- ▶ *clenched fists*
- ▶ *finger-pointing*
- ▶ *eye-narrowing and staring*
- ▶ *hands on hips*
- ▶ *dominating behaviour.*

Performance fright

You would be surprised how many people are scared of speaking in front of others. The fear of making a fool of yourself can be literally disabling and it is often only through training that confidence can be increased and performance improved. If you are a shy, retiring sort of person, the chances are that you will find performing more difficult than your outgoing, self-assured colleagues.

One of the misapprehensions that people have about public speaking is that they are 'alone up there' – having to convince. In fact the audience is already committed just by being there and, if anything, is urging the speaker to do well by giving them the answers they want to hear. In other words you have them in the palm of your hands before you start. So it's not so much about winning hearts and minds, as building on the foundation that already exists.

It stands to reason that if most of what we communicate is non-verbal, then a large part of performance depends upon **presence** and the signals you give to convey your argument. You only have to watch good television presenters to know what this means.

In effect, they 'sell' themselves by connecting with the audience. They use more eye contact than average and their facial expressions and head nods reflect **interest** in the interviewee or audience. Disagreement may be shown through a simple raising of an eyebrow, turning away or leaning back when responding. Gestures, on the other hand, are generally kept to a minimum as these can be distracting.

Interviewers, on the other hand, often deny eye contact, appear frosty-faced and adopt postures which appear non-inclusive. Frequent interruptions are designed to unnerve interviewees, as is the posing of new question before the previous one has been answered. With time limitations dictating how much can be said during the interview, the interviewer's job is to get the interviewee to say as little as necessary, as lucidly as possible. Any verbal or non-verbal strategy that achieves this aim has to be considered.

Rules of engagement

It's interesting that the phrase 'having them in the palm of my hands' symbolizes successful communication. In body language terms, upturned palms are associated with honesty, openness and sincerity. But no matter how honest or sincere a person you are, if you can't communicate this to others, then you aren't performing effectively. Ribbens and Thompson list ten rules for engaging an audience successfully:

1 Maintain eye contact
If you make every member of the audience feel that you are talking to them personally, you will have gone half way to persuading them to support you. This is best achieved by making eye contact randomly, but as widely as possible, so that individuals feel included at all times. Presenters who do this are more likely to be perceived as sincere, credible, experienced, persuasive and friendly.

2 Think about hand gestures and tone of voice

When presenting facts it helps to hold the hands out with the palms facing down, as this indicates assurance and certainty. Speak slowly, varying tone and resonance. This way you won't lose the audience's attention.

3 Repeat key phrases

You can add emphasis by repeating key phrases and sounding assertive as you reinforce your point. You often witness this in speeches by politicians who need to get their message across as confidently and authoritatively as possible.

4 Use visual aids

It's not always easy to maintain eye contact with an audience while speaking, so the use of prompt cards and flip charts can give you the reminders that enable your presentation to flow. But don't be distracted by the visual aid because your body language will show that you have lost touch with the audience.

5 Look and sound professional

Whatever you do, try to limit confirmatory phrases like 'Do you see?', 'Do you know what I mean?', and 'OK?', because this gives the impression that you aren't sure of yourself. Don't fiddle with pens or pointers, and don't stand with your hands in your pockets or wander around while speaking, because this distracts the audience's attention away from what you are saying.

6 Be enthusiastic

Enthusiasm can be infectious as long as it isn't over the top. Audience attention noticeably drops off after a while so try to be upbeat as you proceed. Animated facial expressions, body positions and gestures count for a lot in winning people over.

7 Use natural breaks

To maintain audience attention it is often worth creating natural breaks whereby you pass round literature and other items connected with your presentation. Keep the material hidden from view until then as it can be distracting.

8 Note negative body language

Certain postures and gestures amongst an audience tell you how receptive they are to what you are saying. For example, leaning the chin on a hand with an index finger on the cheek indicates critical appraisal or evaluation. 'Steepling' – literally where the fingers of both hands touch and appear to form a church steeple – suggests that people have made up their minds for or against you. When people appear to be picking fluff off their clothes, it suggests that they aren't in agreement with you, but are unlikely to challenge you about it.

9 Avoid distractions

Remember that body language is a two-way process and that it's easy to be distracted by someone else's eye contact, leg-crossing, hair-ruffling or other gestures. The moment your attention is distracted, the audience's attention will wane.

10 Encourage participation

If audience attention is flagging, or you feel you need to bring people in to maintain their attention, you can always mention their names, refer to something over which they have responsibility, or ask for questions and comments. If you are sitting around a table, changing your posture may help to 'loosen things up', particularly since people tend to echo or mirror the actions of a good presenter.

Making the connection

Nursing is an occupation in which body language is important because patients need comfort and reassurance. When you are feeling unwell, or are apprehensive about the outcome of an operation, the last thing you need is an unsympathetic nurse who makes you feel you are a burden. All it takes to make you feel at ease is the sense that you are important and not just a number on a ward. If you think about it, the things that help to put you at your ease are positive affirmations of caring, like smiles and eye contact, attentive listening signified by head-nods and encouraging sounds ('mm-hmm', 'mmm', oh'), open gestures, a gentle lean forwards, physical closeness, a sensitive touch (e.g. hand-holding, arm around shoulder, light hugging) and neatness in appearance.

In general **teachers** are expected to be friendly, warm and rewarding, as well as confident, organized and emotionally stable. They need to interact with, and be attentive to their students, avoiding any appearance of sarcasm, hostility, anger or arrogance. They are also expected to be receptive to cultural differences and to respect variations in attitude towards bodily contact, dress code and personal space. The trouble is that they are also exposed to pressures in the classroom that severely test their tolerance and moderation skills and for this reason an awareness of positive and negative body language is important, not least because of its influence on young people's development.

For example, by maintaining an upright posture, teachers indicate their confidence (rather than dominance) and attentiveness in the classroom. Using expressive gestures enhances what is being said and offers encouragement to others to participate in dialogue. Smiles provide reassurance and indicate approval, as well as showing willingness to interact. Maintaining eye contact is essential during classroom interaction, as is awareness of tone, pitch, volume and rate of speech in different situations. A dull monotone or an uninterested delivery simply alienates student from teacher, so anything that can be done to hold students' attention in this respect can only be a good thing. Remember, it's not necessarily what you say, but the way that you say it that counts.

Being a **pop star** is not normally regarded as an occupation, yet pop stars often work a lot harder than the rest of us. What may look like pleasure can frequently be more arduous than glamorous. Their body language on stage, or camera, often requires prolonged eye contact with the audience, sometimes in a deliberately flirtatious manner. Facial expressions, both on and off stage, tend to be exaggerated. Smiles are broader and scowls are used for effect. Deliberately provocative head movements, and accentuated gait, add dramatic effect. Appearance is often unconventional, bordering on the bizarre in extreme cases, but this has more to do with *performance* than normal everyday behaviour. It is only when the images conveyed by performers filter down into society itself that Life starts to imitate Art.

Most occupations have their own body language requirements. **Receptionists** need welcoming facial expressions, extended eye contact and a pleasant manner to respond effectively to clients, as well as to gain the attention of managers. **Retail sales personnel** need to anticipate the interests of potential buyers – something that special training can improve. A smart appearance and confident (not cocky) approach to customers are essential. A casual approach evidenced by a slouching posture, an unsmiling face, or a vacant look, means 'I can't be bothered'.

The same applies to **sales professionals** for whom eye contact needs to be dominant rather than submissive. In sales, affirmatory head movements, close proximity and bodily contact – whenever this can be achieved without awkwardness and embarrassment – count for a lot. Gerard Nierenberg and Henry Calero observed that, when trying to negotiate a sale, people tend to buy more readily from someone physically closer to them than someone who remains at a distance, hence, many salesmen use visual aids that enable them to 'close the gap' between themselves and the prospective buyer. If the buyer then reacts defensively (e.g. by folding his or her arms) the salesperson knows to move away until the buyer relaxes.

Signalling a willingness to co-operate in a negotiating situation can be achieved in a number of ways:

▶ **Sitting forward** *on a chair can communicate both interest and a desire to agree with others.*
▶ **Unbuttoning the jacket** *can signal an opening up to other people.*
▶ **Cocking the head** *can be interpreted as communicating intent.*
▶ **Steepling** – *where both hands are placed together like a church steeple – with fingertips touching and the palms a short*

distance apart, signifies that the prospective buyer is weighing up the situation and may be close to a decision.

Figure 4.1 Steepling.

On the other hand, **drumming** with the fingers, **tapping** with the feet, and **doodling** indicate boredom, impatience and a waning of interest.

Negative body language of this kind can prejudice the success of negotiations, so action needs to be taken promptly to re-engage the buyer (most people do not drum or tap when talking).

Business executives rely on positive body language. Here though, facial expressions tend to be more neutral, moderated by smiles on greeting and parting. Head movements also tend to be more restrained, with affirmatory responses being subtler than in sales contexts. A reason for this is that in many situations business executives have to hold their cards close to their chests. Body language can so easily give things away, so it is necessary for them to be aware of it as much as possible. One of the most important lessons the business communicator needs to learn is to synchronize his or her use of body language to that of the people with whom business is being done. This is because **posture congruence,** as distinct from mimicry, has been shown to make a difference in business outcomes (see Chapter 9).

It is worth studying business meetings to identify the kinds of individuals who most frequently succeed in gaining the floor. Often they are the ones who maintain eye contact with the chairperson, indicating their wish to speak by leaning forward and raising an index finger. Sensitivity to timing can enable someone who wants to speak to cut in just as the previous speaker is finishing, without giving the impression of interrupting. Once having gained the attention of the audience, eye contact with individual members is made in sequence – reinforcing their sense of inclusion, as well as providing feedback on how well the speaker's points are going down. The confident speaker uses facial expressions and gestures that indicate the direction he or she is moving on a given topic. After all, the aim is to convince, so everything about those few minutes in front of the audience needs to be convincing.

The one person who can make effective use of body language is the chairperson. He or she can achieve many things non-verbally, such as preventing someone from speaking simply by denying eye contact, or showing disapproval of what is being said by turning away from the speaker. The use of head nods can both encourage someone to keep on speaking, or suggest to them that it's time to stop. So much for the impartiality of the chair!

CONFIDENCE AND TEAM BUILDING

One of the most noticeable characteristics of effective teams is how many of the members share similarities in appearance, values and body language – which tends to support the old adage that 'birds of a feather flock together'. Warren Lamb observed that if people are to be welded together into effective teams, it helps considerably if their use of postures and gestures match, or are at least complementary. This doesn't mean being a copycat or that everyone has to be the same. Sometimes opposite poles attract – that is, a dominant and a submissive person can get along very well together because their body language dovetails. Dominant people like to control and regulate interaction; submissive people will happily allow this and may actually welcome it because it removes the necessity for them to make active decisions when they would far rather be passive.

If you are to have confidence in your presentational abilities you first of all need to feel motivated. This involves understanding the nuances of body language in order to create the kind of climate in which others will respond positively to your presence.

Exercise 4: Anticipatory scanning techniques

The next time you are in a public place where people are being served or attended to in some way in sequence (e.g. a bar, cafeteria, airline check-in desk or supermarket checkout), study the people who are working there. Look for examples of anticipatory scanning, such as looking ahead to the next person or persons to be dealt with while still attending to the person at the head of the queue.

Do those who use anticipatory scanning techniques seem to be better at their jobs than those who do not? Note what forms anticipatory scanning takes and the situations in which it most frequently occurs. What of the people who do not use it at all? How does its absence affect their work? What else do you notice about the use of anticipatory scanning in public contact situations?

EXERCISE REVIEW

You will probably have noticed that it is those who use anticipatory scanning techniques who are good at their jobs. The snippets of information obtained from brief looks ahead enable operatives to adapt their approach to fit the needs of the individual customer. In bars, it can help bar staff to serve more than one person at once – they can be waiting for the money from someone who has just received a drink, be preparing the drink for the next person, taking an order from the next person and identifying the person who will be served after that. At airline check-ins, where there are long queues, those who use anticipatory scanning techniques will be looking for nervous travellers who might need reassurance, or who pose a threat.

If your own job involves public contact of this kind, try to develop anticipatory scanning techniques for yourself. You should find that it not only increases your personal effectiveness but also improves your sense of job satisfaction.

Further exercises and experiments

What's my game?
If you can enlist the participation of a few other people, get them to take it in turns to portray an occupation by using body language alone. The others have to guess what the occupation is. Which kinds of job are easiest to portray non-verbally? Which are the easiest to guess? Are both categories made up of the same jobs?

The ideal workmate
Make a list of the body language characteristics you would look for in an ideal colleague or workmate. Think in terms of eye contact, facial expression, head movements, gestures, postures, personal space, bodily contact, appearance, timing and synchronization, and non-verbal aspects of speech.

How tolerant are you?
Imagine that a new person has just taken the place of a long-term friend and colleague and that they are different in every way from what you have been used to. For example, you are middle-aged, courteous and like having things done in a certain way, and they are young, super-confident and want to shake things up a bit. How would this affect the way in which the group or team you work with operates?

Respect
Observe how football professionals behave during big matches and ask yourself what all the posturing and flamboyant gesturing is all about when a goal is scored. What does this body language tell you? Is it about respect? If so, what does it have to do with footballing skill and effective teamwork? Is it just for show?

Part two
Skills and techniques

The time has come to look in detail at the skills and techniques offered by a greater understanding of body language. An integrated approach to the development of interactive or social skills should contain practical as well as theoretical elements. Practice helps to 'free you up' and make you more receptive to others. It is surprising how sensitive some people are about opening up and sharing themselves, particularly where this involves having to divulge things that normally go unsaid. So by undertaking the exercises and experiments in this section, and keeping a record of your responses, you will not only provide yourself with valuable feedback, but also increase your confidence in relating to others.

5

Eye contact

In this chapter you will learn:
- *the importance of eye contact in non-verbal communication*
- *what we are doing with our eyes and how they work to our advantage*
- *why eye contact is such a significant body language skill.*

Eyes are truly amazing. They tell you things you might never learn through speech. They are beguiling, powerful, disconcerting, bewildering, reproving, supportive and loving – and they encapsulate what we mean by face-to-face communication.
We say, 'a single glance can speak volumes' because in a flash we understand something that words cannot convey. Eye contact is, arguably, the most powerful means of communication we possess and the power of the eyes is at its greatest when two people are looking directly at each other – literally gazing into each other's eyes.

Experiments have shown that children, in particular, respond to simple drawings of eyes in much the same way they respond to eyes themselves, suggesting that, from the earliest age, they find other people's eyes of compelling interest. They will even respond to circles that look like eyes because it is through them that they first make contact with others. It may well be that such responses are instinctive and connected with basic survival patterns given that youngsters who secure eye contact gain attention and stand a better chance of having their needs satisfied. There is no doubt that as we grow up we learn not to misbehave when an adult is watching us simply by noting the looks on their faces.

Because eye contact differs between children and adults, men and women, introverts and extroverts, and so forth, it is essential to consider the context in which it occurs before attempting interpretations. Even when people are talking on the telephone and cannot see each other, eye movement patterns resemble those in face-to-face communication. In this sense, the eyes are effectively 'windows on the soul' and can teach us a lot about the inner workings of our minds.

Uses of eye contact

Broadly speaking, we establish eye contact when we are:

▶ *seeking information*
▶ *displaying attention and interest*
▶ *inviting and controlling interaction*
▶ *seeking to influence, dominate or threaten others*
▶ *providing feedback during speech*
▶ *revealing attitudes.*

The information we acquire provides us with clues about whether people recognize us, whether they like us or not; whether they are paying attention to what we are saying; what their state of mind is – people who are depressed or introverted, for instance, tend to avoid eye contact – and how honest they are.

Feedback is important when we are speaking to each other, so attentiveness is reassuring, while wandering eyes suggest a lack of interest in what we are saying. As soon as we look at someone, they know they have our attention. If we look at them for longer than a few seconds, they will infer that we are interested in them.

The fact is that eye contact plays a vital role in creating the conditions for rapport. It might be 'love at first sight', or just breaking the ice, but whatever the reason, we *invite* the other person to interact with us. Once this happens we use our eyes to control the nature and duration of the interaction. This also helps us synchronize our responses to each other.

Attitudes are often revealed by the willingness, or otherwise, of one person to provide another with opportunities for eye contact. People who like each other engage in more eye contact than those who do not. Aggression, however, is also signalled by prolonged eye contact – which is why we use the phrase 'eyeball to eyeball confrontation'. On the other hand, shame, embarrassment and sorrow are usually characterized by the deliberate *avoidance* of eye contact.

Other emotions, too, have their individual eye behaviours. When we are excited, our eyes tend to make rapid scanning movements. When we're afraid, they appear frozen open, as if watching for the slightest movement that spells danger. When we are angry, our eyes narrow, often into little more than slits, while sadness has a 'downcast' look where our eyes rarely meet those of others.

We look at the other person more when listening than when speaking and we signal with our eyes when we're ready to give way to them. When saying hello we usually move our eyebrows up and down once. This **eyebrow flash** is a universal indication of recognition and greeting.

Winking is used to indicate that something is not to be taken seriously, or when we're just being friendly, while long, unflickering looks are used to intimidate or influence others. Generally speaking, people don't like to feel threatened so that if this kind of behaviour occurs in situations like negotiations or interviews, it can have an adverse effect on the outcome.

When eye contact is broken, we tend to gaze to the left or right. Observations have shown that when people are posed verbal questions they tend to break gaze to the right and downwards, yet if they are asked spatial questions they tend to break to the left and upwards. There is even some evidence to suggest that left breakers tend to be more artistically inclined while right breakers are more scientifically oriented, relying less on visual imagination than spatial awareness and observation.

What our pupils can teach us

Two intriguing facts about eye behaviour have been discovered in recent years. One is that when we see something interesting our pupils dilate. The other is that we like people with dilated pupils better than those with contracted pupils.

In the first case, Hess found that when a group of people were shown pictures of a baby, a mother and baby, a naked male, a naked female, and a landscape, he found that men's pupils dilated most when looking at the naked female, while women's eyes dilated to the greatest extent when looking at the mother and baby. In the second case he showed people two pictures of the face of an attractive girl. The pictures were identical, but in one the pupils had been retouched to make them appear larger. Almost everyone thought the picture with the enlarged pupils was more attractive, but very few were able to say why. The conclusion was that pupil size determines our responses to different stimuli even though we may not be aware of their effect at a conscious level (see Figure 5.1).

Pupil responses have also been used in opinion polls and market research to measure public attitudes to political candidates and products: the more favourable the attitude, the more dilated the pupils. Because this kind of eye behaviour is not consciously controlled, it can be a reliable indicator of interest, attraction and personal preferences.

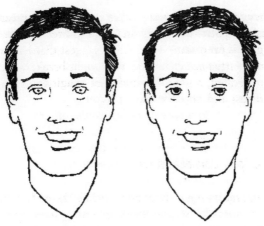

Figure 5.1 Both faces are smiling, but to most people the one on the left appears cold and insincere – what do you think?

Eye grammar

The rules that govern the use of eye contact can be likened to the grammar of spoken language. We are not always aware of it, but we punctuate when we speak by using hesitation, inflexion and emphasis – supported by unspoken gestures. We do similar things with eye contact. It can be long lasting (as when two lovers gaze into each other's eyes) or it can be short (as when looking at someone who does not like being stared at). It can be direct (a bold, full-frontal gaze) or indirect. It can be intermittent (the kind we use in conversation simply to check that the other person has understood us) or continuous (as in a stare).

Most of the rules of eye grammar are dependent on the context in which eye contact occurs. Some, however, are universal – that is to say they have similar applicability in any context, at any time, virtually anywhere in the world. For example:

▶ *too much eye contact signifies disrespect, threat or superiority*
▶ *too little eye contact signifies shyness, lack of attention, impoliteness, insincerity and dishonesty*

- *lowering the eyes is usually taken as a signal of submission*
- *steady, or repeated, eye contact occurs when people are:*
  - *placed far apart*
  - *discussing impersonal or easy topics*
  - *interested in the other and their reactions*
  - *liking or loving the other person*
  - *trying to dominate or influence the other*
  - *extrovert*
  - *dependent on someone who isn't being responsive.*
- *people look at each other less when they:*
  - *are placed close together*
  - *are discussing intimate or difficult topics*
  - *are not interested in the other's reactions*
  - *don't like the other person*
  - *perceive the other person as being of higher status*
  - *are introverted.*

There are also unspoken rules about where we can look at each other and for how long. You don't *stare* at a woman's cleavage, or a man's genital area, because it's embarrassing for the person being stared at. On the other hand you might have a quick glance before averting your eyes. This is because too much eye contact can be very unsettling, and staring is usually considered impolite. The only people who seem to be able to stare openly are young children who are simply showing a healthy curiosity about the world. Even so, parents still tell their children that it's rude to stare.

The mind's eye and NLP

The issue of how we see things *in the mind's eye* has generated a whole new field of enquiry about the relationship between our senses and the way we process information about the world. As we have already seen, the fact that we constantly observe does not necessarily mean that we are *aware* of what we are observing. Nor, for that matter, are we always aware of touching, hearing, smelling, or even seeing. We just *do it*. It's almost as if our subconscious minds run perception software which helps us to make sense of the ever-changing stimuli to which we respond.

It is this recognition of how the mind and the senses interact in perception that gave rise to **neurolinguistic programming,** or NLP for short. Combining elements from disciplines as widely apart as psychology, linguistics and computer science, NLP seeks to enable people to process and understand perceptual information and to use it to improve the way they act and respond in everyday life. Ribbens and Whitear describe these elements as follows:

Neuro refers to the system of nerves that receives and transmits information about our environment to and from the brain, which includes memory storage.

Linguistic refers to both the internal language we use to 'talk to ourselves', as well as the spoken language we use to communicate with others.

Programming refers to the systems we create in our minds that enable us to respond to internal and external stimuli. These are formed out of life experiences and are largely outside our conscious control.

You don't, for example, consciously think about how you clean your teeth, or what route you travel to work every day, because once having logged the information about how to do these things, your 'data banks' store the knowledge and call on it subconsciously when required. What is interesting, however, is that your body language reflects how the 'mind's eye' is working, revealing how you feel, how you are responding to different tasks, and how you perform under different circumstances.

The more skilled you become in recognizing these factors both in yourself and others, the better you become in being able to predict future behaviour. This, in turn, has considerable significance for problem management, performance enhancement and assessment. Much therapeutic work now centres upon improving cognitive and behavioural awareness thanks to the development of techniques drawing on insights gained through NLP and related disciplines.

Visual thinking

It sounds a bit odd to talk about 'visual thoughts', but your eyes actually convey information about the way you are thinking at any given time. NLP research has shown that when we process information our eyes move in different directions according to how we individually perceive the world around us. Some of us see in pictures, some in sounds and some in terms of feelings and emotions. This has led to models being developed for differentiating between each type of 'thinker'. For example:

Visual thinkers often use visual phrases like 'I see that', 'that's quite clear to me', 'we should focus on...', 'this throws light on...' and so forth.

Auditory thinkers use words and phrases that describe sounds, such as 'that sounds good to me', 'it strikes a chord somewhere', 'Listen...', 'it's worth discussing', 'you'll need to articulate more clearly', etc.

Kinaesthetic thinkers often use more emotional language like 'it feels good to me', 'I warm to that', 'it made quite an impact on us', 'that scenario stinks', 'it's getting hard to handle', etc.

What is interesting is that for each type of thinker, eye movements tend to differ in relation to what is being accessed. For example:

▶ *looking upwards indicates that you are thinking visually, as does looking into the distance deep in thought*
▶ *looking sideways to the left or right indicates that you are 'listening' – that is, thinking in sounds*
▶ *looking down indicates that you are examining your feelings about something.*

Figure 5.2 The eyes have it – thinking visually, in sounds and examining feelings.

Additionally:

▶ *looking upwards to the right indicates that you are recalling information, whereas to the left it suggests you are constructing a picture of what you are about to say*
▶ *looking down to the right suggests you are evaluating something or coming to a decision, whereas to the left suggests you are examining your feelings about something.*

Obviously this doesn't mean that all people can be 'categorized' into thinking systems. We all use these eye movements at different times, but there is certainly evidence that we have tendencies to think in one or other of these modes because of our backgrounds and upbringing. Furthermore, like left- and right-handed people, the eye orientation can sometimes be reversed, so it is important to note this before coming to a judgement about how someone is thinking. The best way of doing this is to gain the attention of the person you are about to speak to by looking at them directly and taking note in which direction their eyes move initially when recalling who you are, what your name is and the last time you met.

The power of eye contact in communication is undisputed. To gauge for yourself what forms it takes, the uses to which it can be put, and how effective it is in our contacts with others, try checking out the simple procedures in the following exercise.

Exercise 5: What are they looking at?

Next time you are in a public place, like a bar or a restaurant, observe those around you as discreetly as you can. Note how they look at each other when they are talking. Note how long each period of eye contact is (no need to time it – just note whether the mutual glances are short or long). Do they spend all their time looking at each other or do they look around at the other people present? Do they spend much time looking at objects in the room? How do they react when someone enters or leaves? What kinds of people look at each other the most (and least) when they are talking? How do the patterns of eye contact of people sitting side by side differ from those of people sitting opposite each other? What else do you notice about patterns of eye contact?

Caution: Observe, don't pry. People can react in unpredictable ways to being watched. Think about why. What is it about being watched that is so disturbing?

EXERCISE REVIEW

So what have you found out? If the observations you have made are anything like typical, you will probably have noticed some of the following points:

▶ *When people are talking, they do not look at each other the whole time, but only in a series of glances.*

▶ *In places like bars and restaurants, some time will be spent in looking at those present, especially those who are attractive or who may be behaving oddly (e.g. talking loudly, arguing, drunk).*

▶ *Generally speaking, little attention will be paid to staff members and even confidential conversations will probably continue uninterrupted when staff are within earshot (the same usually happens in places like taxis and chauffeur-driven cars).*

▶ *When people pay more attention to objects in the room, this tends to signify that they are bored with the conversation, new to the place, or are so familiar with each other that little conversation is necessary (or possible).*

▶ *Leaving or entering a room tends to attract attention. Many people who are a little embarrassed about walking alone into a bar or a restaurant forget that this initial curiosity is typical and that it will cease as soon as someone else enters.*

▶ *Those who are having an intimate, personal conversation may look at each other more and for longer than those who are not.*

▶ *People sitting opposite each other will display more eye contact than those sitting side by side. If those sitting side by side desire more eye contact they will turn to face each other.*

> *You will probably not have been conducting this exercise for many minutes before someone has noticed what you are doing, or is at least aware that you are not behaving normally.*

Some of the reasons why people find it disturbing to be watched by someone else are that:

> *the watcher may have the intention of harming you in some way*
> *being watched makes you feel self-conscious and undermines your self-confidence*
> *you may feel they ought to recognize you*
> *you may find the watcher's gaze intrusive, making you want to avoid eye contact*
> *you may be being rather silly, as we often are when in a crowd of friends, and feel that the watching stranger will assume you are always like that*
> *you may think the watcher wants to join your group when this won't be welcomed. The smaller the group, the stronger this feeling can be (e.g. 'Two's company, three's a crowd').*

Further exercises and experiments

So what have we have learned so far to improve our use of this aspect of body language? Certainly developing positive attitudes towards other people requires more effective use of eye contact. If you like people and want to mix more easily with them, it's essential to develop a more outgoing approach. As a rule of thumb therefore:

Be observant
Pay more attention to where other people look and for how long. Note changes in pupil size and the amount of eye contact between individuals.

Engage in more eye contact
See if it increases positive responses. Remember that a direct, open gaze is often preferable to avoidance of eye contact (which may be interpreted by others as shiftiness on our part).

Avoid staring
This can be as inappropriate as refusing to meet someone else's gaze.

Look up when being spoken to
There is nothing worse that someone looking elsewhere when you are talking to them, or vice versa.

Remember, practice makes perfect. What you should do now is to set some time aside over the next few days for practising the following simple exercises:

Staring down
Stare at someone until they look away. Select someone you know well enough to conduct this experiment with, but do not tell them about it in advance. Consider how you feel as you perform the experiment. Ask your subject how he or she felt while being stared at. How long, approximately, was it before they looked away?

Look into my eyes
Select someone you know well and like a lot. Persuade them to sit down with you and look into your eyes for about a minute. Then discuss what you both experienced during the experiment.

Do you like me?
Select an attractive stranger at a party, or somewhere where it's OK for strangers to approach and talk to each other. Try to decide from their eyes alone, as you chat casually, whether or not they like you. Does their willingness (or otherwise) to engage in eye contact affect how well you get on? Observe other couples and try to assess the nature of their relationship from the amount and type of eye contact they engage in.

6

Facial expression

In this chapter you will learn:

- *the significance of facial expressions*
- *the universality of the smile and the 'eyebrow flash' in recognition and greeting*
- *the power of the face in non-verbal communication.*

The study of facial expression has long been a focus of scientific enquiry. Charles Darwin published *The Expression of the Emotions in Man and Animals* in 1872 and other nineteenth-century scientists advanced theories linking body type, cranial shape and facial appearance to intelligence, criminality and even insanity. None has really stood the test of time because physical characteristics are not reliable predictors of behaviour or state of mind. Recent research has indicated, however, that facial expressions do enable us to gain a better understanding of what others are feeling and communicating at any given time.

As with eye contact, we gain a good deal of our information about people's emotional states from the expressions on their faces. Often the face is the first part of a person we look at and so expressions count for a lot in determining attitudes towards us. Pleasure, displeasure, interest, boredom, fear and anger can be clearly read from the way someone looks at us and it is these dispositions that control and shape the way in which we relate to each other.

We make judgements about people on the basis of what we see in their faces. Those with attractive features are often credited with having personality attributes they may not actually possess. 'She's such a lovely person' is more likely to be said about someone with a pretty face, than someone we find unattractive – which is unfair because until you get to know that individual you are relying on looks rather than substance to make the assessment.

The range of expressions

When you consider how many muscles there are in the human face, it is not surprising that the range of facial expressions we can produce is very wide. There are many subtleties in changes of expression – consider, for instance, the variety of smiles observable on the Mona Lisa's face. But is she smiling? You have to make your mind up about what she is conveying. Therein lies the brilliance of Leonardo da Vinci's enigmatic portrait 'La Gioconda'.

In everyday communication facial expressions convey differing degrees of emotion. Ekman and Friesen have noted six which we regularly use to show when we are happy, sad, disgusted, angry, afraid and interested:

▶ **Smiles** *are normally used as a greeting gesture and generally to indicate varying degrees of pleasure, amusement and happiness, though in some contexts they can suggest aggression, sarcasm or doubt. In a smile the mouth is usually closed, but in open smiles the teeth can be showing. A broad smile with the teeth showing is usually called a grin.*
▶ **Downcast looks** *depict sadness, disappointment and depression and are usually revealed by a turning down of the corners of the mouth, eyes pointing downwards and sagging of the features. Extremes of sadness will be characterized by the appearance of tears, trembling of the lips and attempts to shield the face from view.*
▶ **Grimacing** *conveys disgust or contempt and is portrayed by narrowing of the eyes, clenching of the teeth, wrinkling up of the nose, and turning the head aside to avoid having to look at the cause of the reaction.*

- **Fixed gaze** *often characterizes anger and is accompanied by frowning, scowling and gritting of the teeth. Some people go pale when angry, while others go red, or even a purplish colour in extreme anger or fury. Body posture tenses up as if preparing for offensive action.*
- **Wide eyes** *tend to depict fear and can be accompanied by an open mouth and trembling which affects the face as much as the rest of the body. There may even be signs of perspiration and a paleness of colouring.*
- **Cocked head** *shows interest and is often indicated by holding the head at an angle to the subject, accompanied by eyes that are open wider than normal and a slightly open mouth (especially common in children). When seated we tend to prop our chins with our fingers during attentive listening.*

See if you can match facial expression to emotion in Figure 6.1.

Figure 6.1 Can you correctly identify each of the emotions illustrated above?
(A) happiness (B) sadness (C) disgust/contempt (D) anger (E) fear (F) interest

Faces and first impressions

It is said that the most critical period in an encounter between two people is the first five minutes. Impressions formed at this time tend to persist, which is why we often place such importance on 'first impressions'. But in these first few minutes we do more than simply decide whether or not we like someone. We make judgements about their character, personality, intelligence, temperament, personal habits, working abilities, suitability as a friend or lover, and so on. All of this is done on the basis of very little information about the other – and yet we are more often right in these judgements than we are wrong. Ask yourself how often you recall changing your first impression of someone and compare this with the people you know. Try making a mental note of those you meet for the first time and see in a few weeks if you've changed your mind about them.

Talking with your face

We can say quite a lot with our faces. Often we use facial expressions to communicate when words won't work, for example, when someone says something out of place and our faces rather than our voices do the talking. The phrase 'a nod is as good as a wink' captures the sense of mutual agreement facial expressions convey when there is no need to say any more.

The fact is that when we communicate non-verbally, we rely on signals to indicate what we mean and to express our emotional state at that moment in time. A smile tells people we are pleased to see them, a frown warns them off. A downcast look tells them we're not feeling too happy, a raised eyebrow and a twist to the mouth shows we are in playful mood. A head cocked on one side shows we are listening. We shut our eyes to let someone know we have switched off.

We have already seen how the eyebrow flash operates as a gesture of recognition. Rapid up and down movement of the eyebrows, accompanied by a smile, informs the other person that we are pleased to see them. But there are numerous non-verbal judgements we make when meeting, such as whether we approve of what they are wearing, whether a tattoo really was a good idea, whether that beard ought to come off, whether it's time to do something about those teeth – things we wouldn't dream of saying openly. But we have to be careful what our facial expressions betray. Some people are particularly bad at hiding their disapproval, which is why we use phrases like 'looks can kill' and 'she said it with her eyes'. Moral values influence judgements, particularly across the generations. Earrings worn by men were once interpreted as a sign of effeminacy, just as short skirts and plunging necklines have been branded immodest at various times in the last century. One generation's 'thing' is another's fad, and intolerance of difference is easily betrayed by disapproving looks – the non-verbal equivalent of criticism.

Facial expressions can, however, be used to reinforce the impact of verbal messages. When a mother scolds a child her face tells her offspring just how cross she really is. In face-to-face pay bargaining the set of the jaw will often tell you how successfully, or badly, negotiations are going. Frosty faces during polite conversation at official gatherings betray mutual animosity, while hidden anger is suggested by a narrowing of the eyebrows and pursing of the lips (Lambert, 1999). Thus facial expressions convey silent emotions as well as non-verbal approval or disapproval.

Face facts

Different parts of the face express different emotions. Fear is usually looked for in the eyes, as is sadness. Happiness is seen in the cheeks and the mouth as well as in the brightness of the eyes. Surprise is seen in the forehead, eyes and mouth movements, whereas anger tends to envelop the whole face. In fact, when people are communicating, their facial expressions constantly change. When slowed down, footage of these reveals micro-momentary alterations, lasting perhaps a fraction of a second each. And because the camera never lies, you get to see the true emotion in the face that fails to match the pleasantries of speech.

For example, John is saying how pleased he is to see Peter, but frame by frame John's expressions say the opposite.

People tend to talk less, make more speech errors and smile more when attempting to deceive others than when being completely open and honest. More often than not a 'fake smile' will indicate that the whole truth isn't being conveyed. It's hard to hide the body language of deception, particularly in the face, because muscles around the forehead and eyebrows betray one's true feelings. Nurses and doctors often have to conceal from sick patients just how ill they are, but proper training enables them to manage such 'deception' with integrity because the intention is to do good, not harm.

But it's also easy to get things wrong. When a psychologist showed a number of photographs of innocent people to a test group and asked them to allocate such crimes as armed robbery and rape to the different faces, a significant number identified criminality in those faces. Not only does this raise questions about the reliability of witnesses in police identity parades, but it also flags up the importance of understanding the signals we unwittingly give each other, and what these say about our own attitudes, preferences and behaviours.

___

Smile, you'll feel better

Because the smile is probably the most universally used and the most positive facial expression, it will be useful if we examine it in a little more detail here. Smiles are used all over the world to indicate or reflect pleasure or happiness. Even children who have been blind from birth smile when they are pleased. Smiles are also used to show reassurance, amusement and even ridicule. We shall be concerned here with the positive uses to which smiles can be put.

Smiles are rarely used deliberately, but they can be. Experiments have shown that if individuals are asked to smile and are then shown pictures of various things, they are more likely to react positively to them. On the other hand, if they are asked to frown, they react negatively. What this suggests is that, for some reason, the action of smiling predisposes us to respond more positively to stimuli – which tends to support the popular saying 'smile and the world smiles with you'.

Smiles can also be used to mask other emotions. An athlete who loses to an equal competitor will still try to smile bravely to hide his disappointment. A smile may also be a submissive response to ward off another's attack. Those who work in occupations that bring them into contact with the public, such as receptionists or aircraft cabin crew, are trained to use smiles to reassure clients and passengers. Smiling may be used to make a tense situation more comfortable. A smile will tend to call forth a smile from the other person and thus ease away the tension.

The best time to test the power of the smile is when you least feel like smiling, such as when you're feeling down, or getting over illness. Force a smile on to your face and keep it there for as long as possible. Each time the smile disappears, wait a few minutes and then try again. Within a short time, you should notice a distinct improvement in how you feel. This technique doesn't always work, but very often it will and is certainly worth a try. Of all the facial expressions that we use, smiling is the one that pays the greatest dividends in our relationships with others.

Exercise 6: Say it with a smile

When you make that extra effort to smile it is amazing how responsive people become. It doesn't take much to be pleasant to others, though for a lot of people smiling doesn't come easily. The exercise for this chapter, then, is that for the next week at least you should attempt to greet everyone you encounter with a pleasant smile. You do not have to maintain an inane grin on your face. It is sufficient simply to appear genuinely pleased to see them.

Note their reactions. Do they return the smile? Does the encounter appear to proceed better or worse than it would normally do?

Does anyone appear surprised? Or suspicious? Does the encounter last longer or is it shorter than it would otherwise be?

Of the people you meet several times during the week, does there appear to be any change taking place in the relationship between you? Is there any difference in the responses of men and those of women? Or in those of the young and those of the old? Or those of superiors, colleagues and subordinates? Or those of fellow workers in the organization and those of customers or clients?

Note your own reactions. Did you find the exercise easy or difficult? Did you feel at all silly in carrying it out? If so, why? Did you find your attitudes to people changing at all? Did you find yourself spending longer with people you dislike? Did you find yourself disliking them any less? How do you feel when others smile at you?

Try to keep a record of as many of the reactions as you can.

EXERCISE REVIEW

Let us now consider how the exercise has gone. You will in all probability have noticed at least some of the following points:

- ▶ *most people will have returned your initial smile*
- ▶ *most encounters will have proceeded more smoothly than usual*
- ▶ *some will be surprised, others suspicious, for example, 'What's he/she up to?'*
- ▶ *encounters will probably have lasted longer than expected. When you are nice to people, they tend to be nice back to you*
- ▶ *you may well have found that some of your relationships have improved*
- ▶ *young people tend to respond more readily than older people*

- *subordinates and colleagues generally respond better than superiors, though your more positive approach will probably not have gone unnoticed*
- *customers and clients respond more readily than fellow workers.*

Now, how about your own reactions? You may have noticed that:

- *after some initial awkwardness, you found the exercise quite easy to carry out*
- *you didn't feel silly. If you did, you may have been trying too hard and kept the smile on your face a little too long*
- *your attitudes to others are improving and you are becoming more positive*
- *you are spending more time with people you thought you disliked*
- *you like it when others smile at you.*

Further exercises and experiments

Good morning, world!

Try *not* smiling when greeting people you meet in the street. Count how many smile at you. The following morning smile warmly in greeting at everyone you meet. Count how many return your smile. What's the difference? It's surprising how many strangers will smile if you smile first. It's as if they are afraid to take the initiative.

Facial exercises

To develop muscle tone (get rid of flabbiness and a sagging face), try these exercises in front of the mirror for one minute each day. Starting from the face at rest:

- *grin broadly, lifting the eyebrows at the same time*
- *pucker the lips into a tight round 'O'*
- *lift the chin as high as it will go, raise your eyebrows, grin, then pucker.*

Stop frowning

Whenever you have any concentrating to do, place your palm across your forehead. If you find you are frowning, stop it. If you have to move your face at all, try raising your eyebrows so that your forehead creases horizontally rather than vertically. You will find that one result of this exercise is to make you less prone to headaches.

Show your feelings

In front of a mirror, practise each of the following emotions in sequence:

▶ *happiness*
▶ *sadness*
▶ *surprise*
▶ *disgust*
▶ *fear*
▶ *anger*.

If you can secure the co-operation of someone else, see if they can identify each emotion from your expression. Vary the sequence to make the task a little more difficult for them. This exercise will tell you how well you express your feelings. It will also tell you how good your partner is at recognizing emotions. You can reverse roles once your partner has fully grasped the nature of the exercise and you may even be able to involve others. It can also be a fun party game, with points given for accuracy in recognition.

Is your face your fortune?

Collect six photographs of people's faces, one of which should be a well-known attractive film or TV star. Show them to as large a number of people as possible and ask them to rate the attractiveness of each face on a scale of 1 to 10. Do you find others' ratings agree with your own? Do they tend to agree on the most attractive face amongst the six? The exercise should provide some fascinating insights into people's perceptions of others.

7

....

Head talk

In this chapter you will learn:
- *about head movements and how they signal reflections, thoughts and feelings*
- *about their role in social interaction and their importance when listening and communicating.*

If you watch two people talking, you invariably notice that, in addition to the movement of their mouths and changes in facial expression, their heads move around a lot, sometimes backwards and forwards, sometimes shaking from side to side, sometimes seeming to tip over in relation to certain words and phrases. These aren't random movements. Like eye contact and facial expressions they are part of the body language of head talk.

It's worth reflecting that the phrase 'use your head' refers to more than simply thinking sensibly. Head movements are important not only in talking but also in listening. Used properly they can help us to communicate more easily. Used inappropriately, they can adversely affect a relationship with another person. They act as speech markers in social acknowledgements, as gestural 'echoes' (see next chapter), and as indications of our attitudes towards others in encounters. They are, then, capable of much greater versatility and subtlety of expression than might be supposed.

Talking heads

As with other aspects of body language, head movements can be used for a variety of purposes. Consciously or unconsciously they indicate attitudes and preferences, replace speech and provide support for what is being said. For example, when the head is held high and is tilted slightly backward, this may be interpreted as haughtiness or aggressiveness, whereas a lowered head indicates submissiveness, humility or even depression.

Head movements have an important use as speech markers, particularly in public speaking. Slight head nods, sweeps to one side, and chin thrusts add dramatic emphasis to words and phrases. The head can also be used as a pointer: to suggest the direction you want someone – or the situation – to go in. You often see this used by chairs of meetings to indicate who is the next person to speak. Try watching people's heads as they are speaking (television without the sound is a good medium) in order to observe the small but rhythmic movements made by the head in accompaniment to speech. For instance, the end of a sentence is normally marked by a slight downward movement of the head, followed by a momentary pause before rising again.

Touching the head has numerous non-verbal meanings. When people are anxious they often touch the face, hair, mouths and eyes. Touching the nose and stroking the chin usually occur when we are thinking through something, or making decisions. Covering the eyes, ears or mouth suggest that we don't want to know what's coming. When we've done something stupid we often tap or bang the sides of our heads with our fingers, signifying regret and self-blame. And when we are tired, bored, or quietly working something out, we prop our heads up with our hands under the chin or on the side of the face.

Active listening

It's off-putting when the person you are talking to looks away because it makes you think they are not listening to you. The loss of eye contact matters in conversational speech even though we are perfectly capable of listening when facing the opposite direction, or with our eyes closed. Therefore listening must not only be done, it must be *seen* to be done. This is what we call **active listening** – where the position and movement of the head in relation to the speaker is central to good communication.

Holding the head at a tilted angle while listening to the person speaking to you is known as the **head cock**.

Figure 7.1 Two versions of the head cock.

Animals – especially dogs – use it, as do children, who use it to gain attention, as well as to get what they want. It's as if the slant of the eyes adds reinforcement to the non-verbal message – 'please'.

When we are listening to others we tend to copy their head movements unconsciously. It is almost as if we wish to demonstrate a commonality of interest by a shared behaviour. It is also quite common, when listening carefully, to bring the head closer to the person being listened to. The *tête-à-tête*, or head-to-head talk, indicates a desire for closeness – as true for lovers as those whose intellectual interest is heightened by a stimulating speaker.

Listening while sitting down often involves the head being propped by the thumb and the first two fingers of the hand. Whoever is speaking will tend to interpret this as a sign of intelligent interest. On the other hand, if the listener's chin is propped in the palm (and especially if the eyelids begin to droop) it indicates a decreasing interest in what the speaker is saying.

Attentive listening, then, is by no means purely passive. An active use of the kind of head talk just described indicates to speakers that they are receiving your full and undivided attention – or that they are not.

Now you see it

The orientation of your head when looking at people can have a marked effect upon their interpretation of your behaviour. One of the reasons that makes it possible for you to look at someone 'out of the corner of your eye' is that they will expect the focus of your attention to be where you are facing. But if the direction of gaze is too obviously at variance with the direction of the head, or if sideways glances are too long or too frequent, they will be interpreted as uninterested.

Although indirect observation may not always be appreciated, it can also indicate shyness, coyness or even playful interest. Tilting the head to one side can imply that you aren't taking someone, or something, seriously, or as an appealing gesture made in a playful or flirtatious way. It is also used in greetings, accompanied by the 'eyebrow flash', to suggest how pleased you are to see someone.

The head can also be used aggressively. When thrust forward from the shoulders it poses a threat to an opponent, and when used as a head butt it becomes a lethal weapon. Politicians often project their heads downwards in small, sharp movements to add emphasis to particular words and phrases.

Women tend to use the head cock more than men and are often shown in advertisements and magazine pictures with tilted heads to suggest confidence and freedom. Men tilt their heads forward in a greeting nod more than women. In some societies women are expected to lower their heads submissively as a mark of recognition of their status. This used to be the case in Western societies where gender differences dictated social expectations, but female emancipation has all but removed such barriers to social, sexual and political expression.

Give me the nod

According to the context in which it is used, the head nod signifies:

- ▶ *agreement*
- ▶ *approval*
- ▶ *acceptance*
- ▶ *continuing attention*
- ▶ *understanding*.

The strongest nods usually indicate agreement, while slighter nods provide the speaker with feedback on how well they are being understood. The least obvious, and yet in many ways the most effective, use of the head nod is in showing attentiveness, because by affirming interest the speaker is encouraged to continue.

Research has shown that the amount of speech that can be generated in this way is three or four times greater than normal. This is an important finding because it has practical value for assessing the effectiveness of interviews and formal discussions. Refusal by a listener to nod can make the speaker uncomfortable, sometimes resulting in him or her drying up completely without knowing why. Training courses in the use of body language need to take note of affirmatory responses of this kind as they often have an importance quite out of proportion to their apparent significance. Having said this, nodding shouldn't be done for effect. Too much repetition removes the impact – and the sincerity – of the gesture.

Use your head

So what purposes do head movements serve?

▶ **A means of social acknowledgement** *A nod or a tilt of the head is often used as an informal non-verbal greeting, as is a friendly wink.*

▶ **A way of gaining attention** *Throwing the head back repeatedly in a diagonal movement replaces a shout or a wave and means 'come here'.*

▶ **Expressing doubt or reluctance** *Swaying or rocking the head from side to side suggests you are 'weighing up' something. Tossing or shaking the head expresses disdain or haughtiness.*

▶ **Suggesting preference or acceptance** *Winking, accompanied by a short, sharp downward tilt of the head to one side, suggests that something is not being taken seriously. Sharp upward movements of the chin, accompanied by pursing of the lips, suggest positive consideration.*

▶ **Indicating attitudes or states of mind** *Hanging the head can give the impression of submissiveness, humility or depression. Holding the head erect gives the impression of self-confidence as well as good posture.*

Looking at it from another point of view, you could say that the angle of our heads at any given time indicates the 'position' we are taking on something, or how we feel about it at that moment. The following list gives examples of this.

Angle of head	Meaning
Lowered	showing respect
	self-protection
	avoidance
	submission
	acceptance

(Contd)

Angle of head	Meaning
Hang-dog	tiredness
	depression
	humility
	guilt
	concealment
Raised	'hello'
	confidence
	superiority
	showing interest
	questioning
	reflection
	concentration
Nodding	agreement
	approval
	acceptance
	offering encouragement
	emphasizing
Shaking	disagreement
	disapproval
	disbelief
	amazement
Side-tilt	uncertainty
	interest
	curiosity
	calculation
Swivelling	responding to something
	preparing to engage
	breaking off communication
	being surprised by
	displaying disagreement
Indicating	pointing out something
	'your turn'
	avoiding verbal commitment
	marking territory
	showing potential interest in

Exercise 7: Use your head

Try having a conversation with someone you know well and, as they talk, nod your head encouragingly. Do they seem to do more of the talking or less? On another occasion, try not nodding at all. What's the reaction? Next, repeat the exercise with a stranger.

After each conversation, record your impressions. Note down your own feelings about the exercise. Did you find it easy or difficult to do? Which parts were the easiest and which the most difficult?

Consider how other people use nods when they are talking to you. Observe interviewers on television, preferably with the sound turned off. What kinds of things do you notice about nodding behaviour? Do people nod most when talking or listening? Why do you think this is? Are there any other things you notice about the ways people use nods in face-to-face communication?

EXERCISE REVIEW

Now let us look at what you have found. In the first part of the exercise, nodding your head should have encouraged the other person to speak more and for longer. Refusing to nod should have resulted in the other person drying up and ending the conversation very quickly. You should have had the same experiences when conversing with a stranger, except that you may have noticed that the stranger stoppe d talking earlier when head nods were absent. As far as your own feelings are concerned, you will almost certainly have felt more comfortable and at ease when you were allowed to nod. In fact, you may even have found it impossible not to nod at times.

Further exercises and experiments

A nod of encouragement
In observing other people's head talk, can you say whether people nod more when they are listening than when they are talking? Do some people really not listen, yet still nod – as if marking time before they can take over again? Do they nod encouragement to get the other person to open up? If so, what is their motive?

Observing head talk
Think about all the ways in which head movements signal reactions, responses and feelings. Observe those around you at home, at work, on the train, or perhaps talking in the street, to see what messages you can interpret from their head talk. Is it negative or positive? Do they like each other? Do you think they are being honest?

A nod's as good as a wink
Is this true? Think about the difference between the two body language messages. If you wink at someone, does this mean the same as 'giving them the nod'? If not, why do you think we use this colloquial phrase?

Try using your head
If you are reserved in your use of body language, try experimenting with more demonstrative head talk and see how people respond. Even though you may be self-conscious at first, keep trying. You might be pleasantly surprised with the result.

8

Gestures

In this chapter you will learn:
- **the significance of gestures and body movements in communication**
- **about cultural differences of gestures and their meanings.**

When you 'make a gesture towards somebody', you could just as easily be conceding a point as holding your fist up to them. Both are examples of body language, though in the first case you are more likely to be shrugging your shoulders and raising your arms with your palms turned upwards. Gestures permit a degree of expressiveness and subtlety that other aspects of non-verbal communication do not, and it is these that most people think of when they talk about body language.

Several writers have attempted to classify gestures into categories. Michael Argyle has suggested five different functions that they serve:

- *illustrations and other speech-linked signals*
- *conventional signs and sign languages*
- *movements that express emotions*
- *movements that express personality*
- *movements that are used in various religious and other rituals.*

Paul Ekman and Wallace Friesen describe them in terms of:

- *emblems (movements as substitutes for words)*
- *illustrators (movements that accompany speech)*

- ▶ *regulators (movements signalling changes in listening or speaking roles)*
- ▶ *adaptors (movements betraying a person's emotional state, e.g. scratching the head, fiddling with objects, rubbing hands together)*
- ▶ *affect displays (movements that directly reveal emotions, e.g. outstretched palms).*

Essentially, gestures express attitudes, emotions and non-verbal reactions. Argyle quotes a number of conventional gestures that have almost universal meanings. Examples include shaking the fist to show anger, rubbing the palms together in anticipation, clapping as a sign of approval, raising one's hand to gain attention, yawning out of boredom, patting someone on the back to encourage them, and rubbing the stomach to indicate hunger.

Gerard Nierenberg and Henry Calero show that gestures are used in expressing, amongst other things, openness, defensiveness, readiness, reassurance, frustration, confidence, nervousness, acceptance, expectancy, suspicion and the quality of relationships. They are even used in situations in which the other person cannot be seen, as when making a telephone call or using recording equipment.

Observations of people taking leave of each other show that during the final moments of the encounter one person usually breaks eye contact, leans forward and nods frequently before standing. If they are not then released from the encounter, frustration sets in and the whole procedure has to be repeated. So reading the other person's signals correctly is clearly an essential part of successful interaction. It is this richness of silent communication that we shall now begin to explore.

Let your body do the talking

'Body talk' is central to the study of **kinesics** – a term coined by the American researcher, Ray Birdwhistell, who was one of the first to study body motion communication in the late 1940s. A 'kine' is the smallest observable unit of body movement and kinesics refers to the scientific study of gestures and other body movements. Any part of the body can be used to make a gesture and communication is enhanced, or cut short, by non-verbal actions. For example:

▶ *The* **shoulder shrug** *usually conveys the messages 'I don't know', 'I don't care', 'I am doubtful', or 'what else can I do?' – when both shoulders rise and fall together. A single shoulder shrug often means 'so what?' or 'leave me alone'.*

▶ *The* **chest puff** *is commonly only used in a humorous and self-mocking way though it symbolizes pride or achievement and can indicate conceit or arrogance.*

▶ *The* **stomach tense** *says 'I am really fit' or 'I'm not as fat as I look' and is characterized by pulling in the stomach to make it look flatter and firmer.*

▶ *The* **hand prayer** *otherwise known as 'steepling', occurs when the tips of the fingers are placed together in what resembles an attitude of prayer, except that the palms are kept well apart. It is said to signify confidence, or to make others think you feel confident.*

▶ *The* **hand rotation** *often accompanies feelings of uncertainty and confusion, while sudden upward movements of the hands imply annoyance or loss of control.*

▶ *The* **leg cross** *is a 'keep your distance' gesture, particularly for women, because one leg over the other effectively blocks access to that individual. Of course it also has to do with sitting comfortably.*

▶ *The* **foot dance** *is an example of 'leakage' when someone may be trying to conceal something and is not quite succeeding (i.e. in poker), or is bored, or simply thinking about something. Such leakage usually occurs in the lower half of the body, probably because we take more trouble to control things like facial expressions.*

▶ *The* **pelvic thrust** *generally carries sexual overtones, particularly when dancing, or used by performers on stage, or during aerobic sessions in the gym.*

▶ *The* **buttock thrust** *is similarly associated with sexuality, though it can be used to make humorous, rude or obscene gestures.*

▶ *The* **gestural echo** *occurs when one person uses a gesture and others copy it subconsciously. This happens when people*

'synchronize' with each other during mutually positive
interactions. As we shall see in the next chapter, something
similar happens with posture.

Morris's gesture maps

Desmond Morris's ground-breaking work on non-verbal
communication identified commonly used gestures and the
meanings behind them. He and a team of researchers from Oxford
University published a guide to the origins and distribution of
selected gestures observed all across Europe. They found that the
context in which a gesture occurs is all-important because the same
gesture can have different meanings in different places. For example:

▶ *The **fingertip** kiss where the tips of the fingers and thumb*
  are kissed and then the hand is moved quickly away from
  the mouth and the fingers spread out. It is symbolic of the
  mouth kiss, which is a gesture used all over the world to show
  affection. The gesture is most commonly used to indicate
  praise in Spain, France, Germany and Greece. In Portugal,
  Sardinia and Sicily it is used as a greeting. Its use is relatively
  rare in the British Isles and in Italy.
▶ *The **nose thumb** has the thumb placed on the end of the*
  nose and the fingers fanned out and sometimes waggled.
  It is generally used as a gesture of mockery or insult.
▶ *The **fingers cross** has the first and middle fingers twisted*
  around each other and the remaining fingers held under the
  thumb. It signifies protection, as when someone tells a lie and
  they cross their fingers in the superstitious belief that this will
  prevent them being found out. This meaning is most common
  in the British Isles and Scandinavia, whereas in Turkey the
  gesture is used to break a friendship. Elsewhere it is used to
  indicate that something is OK, to swear an oath, and even as a
  symbol for copulation.
▶ *The **eyelid pull** is when the forefinger is placed on the*
  cheekbone and pulled down to open the eye a little wider,

meaning 'I am alert' in France, Germany, Yugoslavia and Turkey. In Spain and Italy, it means 'Be alert'. In Austria, it was found to signal boredom.

▶ *The* **nose tap** *when the forefinger taps the side of the nose, conveys complicity, confidentiality or an instruction to maintain secrecy in the British Isles and Sardinia. In Italy, it means 'Be alert'. If the tap is to the front of the nose, it can mean 'Mind your own business' in the British Isles, Holland and Austria.*

▶ *The* **thumbs up** *is universally known as the hitch-hiker's request for a lift, as well as a signal that 'everything's OK'. However Morris found that in parts of Belgium, Sicily, Sardinia, Malta or Greece, the gesture could be interpreted as a sexual insult.*

Peoplewatching

Observing people's behaviour can be a fascinating exercise, particularly when you realize how we continually signal things to each other through body talk. Many species in the animal kingdom do this, but as Desmond Morris pointed out in *The Naked Ape*, our animal-like qualities evolved differently from our nearest primates to meet the challenges of life as hunter-gatherers in competition with the animal kingdom. Conscious awareness and speech may have given Homo sapiens the edge in the struggle for survival, but we have never lost the animal-like quality of signalling our feelings, desires and preferences through actions rather than words.

In *Peoplewatching* Morris observed that some of these behaviours have symbolic and ritual qualities. For example, **preening** can involve stroking one's hair, re-applying make-up, straightening one's tie or picking lint off clothing, while **courtship readiness** is signalled by increased muscle tone, facial alertness and upright posture. You may not be aware that you are doing these things, but by doing them you are literally 'making yourself more appealing'. Similarly, **flirting** can involve surreptitious glances, ostentatious arching of the torso, revealing leg crosses and forward leans – all of which subtly, or unsubtly offer an invitation to get to know you better.

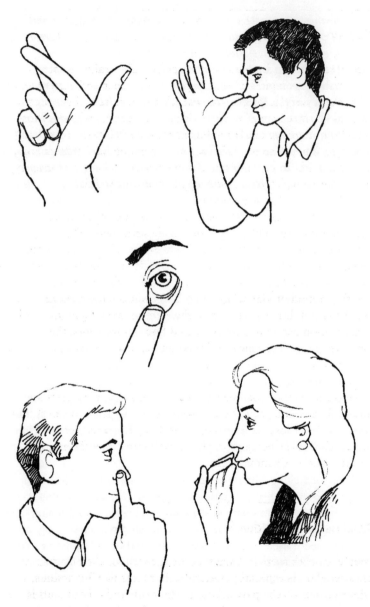

Figure 8.1 Some common gestures.

Gesture psychology

Gestures reflect attitudes as well as personality traits. In fact, personality has a marked effect upon the number and variety of gestures we use. People who use a lot of non-verbal gestures tend to be rated as warm, agreeable and energetic, whereas those who do not are seen as being less approachable, more logical and analytic. What this tells us is that movement equates with energy, so if you want to give an impression of drive and enthusiasm, say, in an interview, let your gestures enhance your words.

Also, we rely on gestures to help us understand other people's personalities and to blend in more easily with them. This is particularly the case with **gestural synchrony** where, as a person listens, their bodily movements seem to echo the rhythms of the other's speech. The listener appears to follow the same 'tune', creating a kind of 'dance' in which speech and movement are synchronized. It has been shown that where two people in conversation use similar gestures and body movements, they perceive themselves as being similar and warm to each other more easily.

In general, the more open and positive you are in your gestures and body movements, the more persuasive you are. Openness and confidence in movement are consistently rated by participants in experiments as being more influential than closed or hesitant gestures and body movements.

Actions speak louder

People at work seem to have their own codes for the meanings of gestures. This is especially noticeable in places like TV studios, where silence on the part of non-participant studio floor staff is essential. The advantages of gestures are that they enable contact to take place without words and act as a kind of convenient shorthand in communication. However, they are limited by the amount of information they can convey. Certain things cannot be communicated by gesture alone (try explaining your name and address by gestures alone), and in some contexts they can simply be unsuitable (e.g. to warn someone of impending danger).

If you observe people of different languages trying to converse, you will almost certainly have noticed that they rely heavily on gestures. Basic needs like hunger and thirst are easier to communicate than complex or sophisticated ones. Some messages may be so long and involved as to defy communication by gesture at all. Generally speaking, nouns and verbs translate more easily into gestures than adjectives, adverbs and other words.

So what are the main points to remember about the use of gestures in self-expression?

▶ **Context** *When using gestures try to be aware of the context in which they occur. Bear in mind that people from different parts of the world may understand a gesture to mean something quite different from what you intend. Avoid gestures which are open to misinterpretation.*

▶ **Be observant** *Note how other people use gestures. Like all forms of body language they can provide a very informative accompaniment to what is actually being said. Much about a person's personality can be inferred from how they gesture.*

▶ **Synchronize** *Note how speech rhythms and body movements relate. Synchronize with, but don't copy, their actions. Be sensitive to the signals they are giving you. Gestural echoes can indicate a sense of identity or sympathy with a group, provided they don't appear too obvious.*

▶ **Be open** *Gestures and body movements convey warmth, trust, and friendliness. Words may be the primary persuaders, but open body language counts for just as much in successful encounters. Negotiators and sales professionals take note.*

▶ **Be natural** *Take your time. Reflect on what is taking place. Allow your gestures to reflect your confidence (or otherwise) in those you are interacting with. For example, steepling conveys a sense of general assurance when listening.*

Exercise 8: Actions speak louder than words

Find a situation that you can observe where people cannot communicate with each other by using words, because it is too noisy, because silence is necessary, because they are too far apart to hear each other, or because there is some other barrier to spoken communication. Examples might include a noisy factory, a TV studio, a restaurant, a building site, a hospital, a library or an examination hall. Look for, and note down, gestures used in such contexts to attract attention, to direct, to tell someone there is a telephone call for them, to beckon, to greet and bid goodbye, to indicate passage of time, to keep quiet, and to convey any other messages that gestures can be used for.

What similarities and differences do you notice? What examples of special codes do you come across? How successful do gestures seem to be as a means of communication? What are their advantages? What are their limitations? How useful are gestures when communicating with someone who does not speak your language? What kinds of needs or requests can most easily be conveyed by gestures? Which are the most difficult to express? Which are impossible to express? How well do words translate into gestures? How well can gestures express emotions? How well can they express or request detailed information?

EXERCISE REVIEW

Where you noticed similar gestures being used in widely different contexts these will have been 'universal' gestures of the kind referred to earlier. You were probably aware that gestures become more deliberate and even exaggerated with increasing distance between those involved, or that gestures used indoors are more controlled and subtle than those used outside. Did you note any differences between gestures used during daytime and at night, or those used at work and in leisure contexts?

Did you observe gesture differences between men and women, adults and children, or people from different social classes?

Further exercises and experiments

The poker player
Observe a group of people playing poker or some other card game. Try to arrange it so that you can see at least one player's hand. Watch for gestures and body movements when a player gets either a particularly good or a particularly bad hand. Tell-tale behaviour will probably be easiest to observe when playing for reasonably significant money stakes.

Everyday mime
Observe situations in which words are an inadequate means of expression. Examples might be when two people are very much in love, when someone has suffered a bereavement, is especially grateful for assistance or a favour, has won a lot of money or won a sporting contest or race. List the gestures that are used to communicate the feelings being experienced. Why are words alone so inadequate in such situations?

Opening up
Practise open gestures such as unfolded and open arms, palms-outward gestures and uncrossed legs. How do others respond? How do you feel about using such gestures? You should be able to communicate with others without feeling you have to fold your arms or cross your legs before you feel comfortable or 'safe'.

Male and female
List as many examples as you can find of gestures that are used exclusively, or predominantly, by men and/or women. What kinds of gestures appear to be used equally by men and women?

Gestural favouritism

Observe your friends' gestures. What is each one's favourite gesture? Head-scratching? Chin-stroking? Ear-pulling? Nose-touching? Arm-folding? Wrapping one leg tightly around another in a kind of double leg cross? Licking the lips nervously? Do you know what your own most characteristic gesture is? You could always ask your best friend to tell you.

9

Posture

In this chapter you will learn:
- *about the role of posture and stance in body language*
- *how posture is an indicator of state of mind during communication.*

Gestures and postures are closely related. We each have a repertoire of postures that we characteristically use to **project ourselves** and it is possible to recognize people we know at a distance from the postures they use. In this sense, posture is a clue to personality, temperament and intention. Think how different an impression someone with an upright posture gives compared to someone who slouches, or how a casual lean in your direction can indicate a preparedness to get to know you better.

There are three main kinds of posture:

- ▶ *standing*
- ▶ *sitting*
- ▶ *lying down.*

Obviously there are many variations on these and we shall concern ourselves here with the first two only. Depending upon the different positions of the arms and legs and the various angles at which the body may be held, you can read a lot about someone's state of mind.

Most individuals have what Birdwhistell calls 'preferred postures'. These are said to reflect a person's past. For example, people who have gone through prolonged periods of depression may still retain a hunched or stooping posture even years after they have recovered and resumed normal lives. Those who faced bullying, or were made to 'stand up for themselves' as children, may exhibit curved, defensive postures. So by becoming aware of postural patterns we may be able to alter our **stance** thereby improving our ability to maintain positive, communicative relationships with others.

Mood signatures

You can't tell what someone is thinking simply from observing their posture, but you can certainly gauge their general state of mind – whether they are happy, sad, confident, shy, dominant or submissive. These are the 'signatures' we leave by our presence and, for this reason, posture observation is useful in determining the most productive approach to make to another person. Postures also have the advantage that they can be accurately observed at some distance, unlike facial expressions where a greater degree of proximity is necessary.

Albert Mehrabian's work on posture has shown that attitudes and status are reflected in the stances we take towards others. For example:

▶ **Positive** *attitudes towards others tend to be accompanied by leaning forward, especially when sitting down.* **Negative** *or hostile attitudes are signalled by leaning backwards. When the arms are folded across the chest this signals inaccessibility, indifference or dislike, whereas if they are relaxed by your side this usually signals openness and a willingness to interact.*
▶ **Insiders and outsiders** *When people are standing around talking in groups, those who are really 'in' the group often display quite different postural patterns to those who are not. Outsiders typically stand with the weight on one foot, whereas insiders will lean forward a little with head tipped forward.*

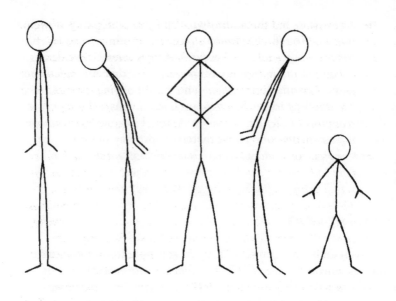

Figure 9.1 What do these postures tell you about the people concerned?

- ▶ **Aggression and threat** *are signalled by an upright 'challenging' posture. The forehead may appear to jut out in front (as if to butt anyone who seriously challenges them). Threatening behaviour often displays exaggerated or dominant behaviour, as if to say 'I'm better than you'. Fist-clenching is an extreme example of threat, though bodily tension generally signals a readiness for action. A tense individual is to be feared more than someone who is relaxed.*
- ▶ **Cool vs. cocky** *People who are comfortable with each other tend to have matching postures. For example, if one person stands with his hands in his pockets, the other will, too. The same applies to leg-crossing and uncrossing. Sometimes, however, a too-relaxed posture can be interpreted as cocky, especially in contexts where sitting up straight might be expected (as in a disciplinary interview). Extreme relaxation of posture can signify a lack of respect for authority.*
- ▶ **Submissiveness and humility** *are suggested by a cowering, slouching posture, while closed body positions may also reflect a sense of lower status. Feeling lower than someone tends to make people lower their heads – as if bowing – and seeking to make themselves look smaller. By comparison, people who consider themselves to be of high status often have a more upright posture with the head held high and hands clasped behind the back.*

Body image

Posture reflects body image. The more confident you are the more upright and mobile you appear. The less confident the less open and welcoming you seem. Self-presentation matters whether you are in the public eye or just a member of the public. Actors and politicians undertake training in order to present themselves effectively to their respective audiences. But there is a difference between acting and putting on an act. Sometimes, for the sake of clarity or dramatic emphasis, exaggerated postures and gestures work. But you have to be believable. Failure to do so results in a negative impression being given and no amount of exaggeration will make up for an unconvincing performance.

As an extreme example of this, drunken behaviour gives the impression of being out of control, even though the person drinking may think they are in control of themselves. The exaggeration of normal postures and gestures, while amusing at first, soon becomes embarrassing and even threatening as they increase. This is because our expectations of what we consider normal are challenged by the incongruity of what we are experiencing. The lurching gait, flailing arms and loss of balance conflict with the body image of self-control – vertical lines of sobriety giving way to curved (then horizontal) lines of inebriation.

Confidence is a visual thing. The girl who walks down the road staring at the ground, with her arms wrapped tightly around her chest, suggests defensiveness and a wish to remain unseen. Her slightly bowed posture and closed body language give the impression of low self-esteem. By comparison women are continually presented with advertising images depicting smiling girls with upright postures and open gestures, suggesting that this is the role model to which confident women should aspire.

The fact is that the way we project ourselves indicates how we feel about ourselves. Some people who are said to have 'presence' exude confidence (even if it's an act) and exhibit fewer changes in posture and use of gestures than most of us. This quiet calm is often associated with status and prestige, as if they have that certain *je ne sais quoi* – the unknown factor which distinguishes specialness from ordinariness.

Postural give-aways

There are certain give-aways with postural body image:

► **Folded arms** *indicate withdrawal, defensiveness, self-protection and closure. 'Self-wrapping' is particularly common amongst women.*

- ▶ **Hunched shoulders** *where the shoulders appear to hunch up and the palms of the hands face outwards, indicates uncertainty, perceived threat, helplessness and inadequacy.*
- ▶ **Arms akimbo** *where you stand hands-on-hips with elbows turned out, is a posture of superiority, indicating dominance. It is often adopted in the presence of individuals perceived to be of lower status, for example, in business contexts.*
- ▶ **Walking tall** *gives the impression of uprightness, honesty and self-confidence. It is a way of showing that you feel good about yourself and that you are not afraid.*
- ▶ **Head prop** *where the head appears to be propped up on one hand with the index finger pointing up over the cheek, indicates positive interest.*
- ▶ **Four cross position** *where you sit with the ankle of one leg resting on the knee of the other, hands clasped behind the neck with elbows outstretched, also suggests superiority. Men often do this to reinforce an image of confidence and authority.*
- ▶ **Postural conflict** *which occurs when people deliberately adopt postures different from those assumed by others, is usually done to mark the boundaries of an interaction, or place 'distance' between one person and another. Arms and legs are positioned in such a way as to suggest that intruders are not welcome.*
- ▶ **Postural echoing** *such as clasping hands, folding arms and crossing legs in unison with the other person suggests a high degree of rapport.*

I'm inclined to like you

People who like each other have a habit of leaning towards each other – as if they are literally *inclined* to do so. Also a **sideways lean** when seated generally indicates relaxation as well as friendliness. However, it has been observed that women tend to lean away to the side when in the company of people they dislike, while men remain upright with other men they dislike.

Body shifts occur when people of the opposite sex are conversing and can be a form of courtship behaviour designed to enhance sexual attraction. For example, shifting one's seating position to face, or sit alongside the other person, arching the back and stretching, leaning inwards, stroking or twizzling the hair – are all ways of maximizing one's best assets.

In fact sexual invitation can be indicated by posture. Women may lean forward and bring their arms closer in to the body to enhance their cleavages. Men often stand in the 'cowboy stance' with thumbs hooked over trouser waists or into pockets and fists loosely clenched, giving the impression of cool availability.

Thus, posture is an important indicator of your inclination towards others. While facial expressions may tell you more about emotions, posture suggests the intensity of those emotions.

Exercise 9: Walking tall

Try walking with your body erect, your shoulders straight and your head held high. Don't stretch yourself up artificially, but don't allow your body to sag, your shoulders to become rounded or your head to hang. The easiest thing to do is to look ahead rather than down at the ground, keeping your shoulders back and your stomach in. Just put as much effort into this as you feel necessary.

After you have practised doing this for a few days, consider how you feel. Do you feel any different? Do you feel more positive and confident? Do you feel more relaxed? Do you feel physically fitter? Do you find you are moving about a little more quickly? Do you notice more of what is going on around you? Do you find yourself thinking quicker and more clearly? What else do you notice about yourself?

Then, consider how other people react and respond to you. Do they seem warmer and more friendly? Do they seem more ready and willing to interact with you? Do you find yourself getting more of your own way in encounters with others? Do they comment at all upon your bearing and comportment? Are there any negative responses to your more erect posture? Do you notice any other changes in other people's behaviour towards you?

EXERCISE REVIEW

If you're not accustomed to 'walking tall' – moving around with an erect posture – you will probably have noted a number of things from this exercise:

▶ *it was quite difficult to do from the outset*
▶ *you began to feel more confident in your everyday activities*
▶ *you feel physically fitter and walk a bit faster without feeling you are hurrying*
▶ *you notice more of what is going on around you*
▶ *your thinking is clearer.*

As far as the reactions of others are concerned, you should be finding that they appear to be responding to you with greater warmth and friendliness and that they are more willing to interact with you. You might find that your point of view is accepted more readily than before and that people comment on how 'together' you look. But don't overdo it. The thing is to appear natural and comfortable and not to put on an act.

Further exercises and experiments

Have you the inclination?

Next time you are sitting talking to someone you know well, try leaning slightly towards them. You should notice that this encourages them to talk more, makes them feel you are more interested in what they have to say and generally results in a more satisfactory encounter. Then, on an occasion after that, try leaning back and away from them. You should notice that they tend to talk less, feel you are less interested in them and show signs of not being completely happy with the way the encounter is being conducted.

I am your mirror
Observe how, in encounters in everyday life and on TV, the participating individuals copy or echo each other's postures. Compare situations in which echoing is present with those in which it is not. You should find that, where there is evidence of echoing, the interaction proceeds more smoothly, there appears to be a better relationship between participants and the whole event looks more natural. Conversely, where echoing is absent, you should notice signs of friction, more disagreement and a general sense of people being ill at ease. If you try to use postural echo, do it as unobtrusively as possible.

Sit up straight
Try sitting up reasonably straight in some encounters and deliberately slouching in your seat in others. Note the reactions of others to this behaviour. You should find that they respond more positively to you when your posture is upright rather than when it is slouched.

Out of control
Observe the behaviour of people who are getting drunk and note how others respond to them. Some people will be amused at first, but most will tend to avoid contact if they can. Note the changing postures of the ones who are drinking. As they start to 'fall about' their actions become unpredictable, even threatening.

Open and closed
Practise closed postures by crossing your legs, crossing your arms in front of the body, turning your body away from the people you're speaking to, and using blocking postures to prevent others entering an interaction. Then practise being open by facing people and leaning towards them slightly. Note how they react differently to your greater openness.

10

Personal space and orientation

In this chapter you will learn:
- *about the concept of personal space and territoriality in human behaviour*
- *about the concept of defensible space.*

When was the last time you got really irritated by someone's iPod disturbing your peace and quiet, or people standing too close to you on the subway? What about your line of sight being blocked by a man who keeps staring at you, or not being able to get to the doors because some big kid's legs are in the way? Do you feel cooped up and claustrophobic or just plain angry?

Space invaders

These are just some of the questions that the *New York Times* posed its readers in a recent article about personal space. Questioning why we feel hostile towards people who crowd our lives, it examined the relationship between what we perceive to be our own territory and the invasion of it by others. With urban environments everywhere becoming increasingly dense, people need ways of separating themselves from the masses in order to protect their personal space and privacy. Citing American proxemics research, the article refers to an 'invisible force field' that keeps human beings apart from each other when crowded together.

What we tend to do if someone is standing too close is firstly to avert eye gaze, then turn away, retreat into corners and put whatever distance is available between ourselves and strangers. We don't think about it, we just do it.

According to scientists, personal space involves not only the invisible bubble we create around ourselves, but all the senses. Physical proximity, unwelcome sound, uncomfortable eye contact and smell all constitute invasion, and our unconscious reaction is to counter it in any way that we can. Commuters on packed trains will hold newspapers in front of them to shield themselves from strangers. People in crowded lifts will study the illuminated floor numbers rather than look at each other. Students in college libraries have been observed to pile books up around them in order to shut others out and restrict eye contact. We do these things to limit intimacy with those we don't choose to know, and woe betide anyone who tries to burst the bubble.

Robert Sommer defined personal space as 'that area around each of us which we do not like others to enter except by invitation or under certain special circumstances.' In crowds we are prepared to accept less personal space than normal. Sometimes this is deliberately invaded by others, which can be unsettling. The point is that if 'closeness' is uninvited it is almost always perceived as threatening. Where the threat potential is highest, body orientation is at its most direct. Crowded conditions create situations in which people behave differently from normal. In lifts, on public transport and at football matches people usually avoid face-to-face contact. Where crowding is so severe, such as on commuter trains, defensive positioning will take place so as to restrict bodily contact. This results in people standing or sitting rigidly staring into space, making as few movements as possible and avoiding all eye contact with others as if to say 'leave me alone, this is my space.'

Ultimately, choice is a key issue in personal space. You choose whether you want to sit in a crowded cinema to watch a film you really want to see, and you choose to dance side-by-side with strangers at a music venue. On the other hand you probably don't feel you have any choice about going to work on packed trains and buses, or fighting your way to the checkout in your local supermarket after a full day's work. Despite all this, it is rare for people to get into confrontation over personal space. We avoid each other and create buffer zones between ourselves and others, and we privately seethe at the people who make us feel uncomfortable.

My space, my territory

When personal space is violated, people tend to move away from intruders, yet maintain a direct orientation towards them – to make the point that their presence isn't welcome. If the intrusion persists, one's orientation changes accordingly to emphasize the boundaries within which invasion of privacy will not be tolerated. In other words, we use body language as a territorial marker. As we have already said, it is possible to sit at an angle in such a way as to close people off – by stretching the legs out, for example. In fact, the angle of orientation can regulate the degree of privacy in a conversation. When you are exchanging confidences you don't want people to hear, you turn away in order to limit intrusion.

This sheds an interesting light on human territoriality. Sommer's studies of the space people need for peaceful living found that housing design significantly affects the way people get on with their neighbours. He developed the idea of defensible space to describe the area we feel we need to protect against unwanted intrusion by others. For example, if flats are too small, or are too closely packed, tensions arise which can spill over into open hostility. But this depends on what one is used to. In Hong Kong, where population density is far higher than most Western cities, people have adapted to having limited living space. When asked what the effect would be of increasing the living space allowance, Sommer was told by the housing authority that, given more space, tenants would just sub-let.

Planners understand the importance of personal space, particularly in areas where people congregate in large numbers, such as shopping precincts. How we move through public spaces, where we stop to look, what type of restaurants we like eating in, what colours and furnishings we find most comfortable – these are all factors which influence our sense of freedom and space. It has been found that shoppers will walk away from whatever they are looking at if their space is compromised, if they are distracted by intrusive staff, or if their concentration is disturbed by other shoppers.

Comfort zones

How physically close we are to people, and whether we face them or not during an encounter, can significantly affect the way in which we get on together. Edward Hall, the father of proxemics – the study of the use of space in communication – identified four spatial zones in which we operate:

▶ **The intimate zone** – *from zero to one and a half feet (0–0.5 m), in which we actually touch or are easily able to touch each other.*
▶ **The personal zone** – *extending from one and a half to four feet (0.5–1.2 m) in which we are no more than an arm's length of each other.*
▶ **The social-consultive zone** – *from four to ten feet (1.2–3 m), most commonly used in everyday encounters of a social or business nature.*
▶ **The public zone** – *from ten feet (3 m) outwards.*

Learning to use personal space more effectively can make a lot of difference in our day-to-day contacts with others. An experiment carried out by James Baxter and Richard Rozelle into the effects of crowding on communication skills, found that the more crowded or pressurized we feel, the less well we function. They selected two groups of people, both to be interviewed by someone playing the role of a police officer. The first group was subjected to intimidating face-to-face interviewing, whereas the second was allowed slightly more space to respond.

Both groups were quizzed about the contents of their wallets. The officer initially stood four feet (1.2 m) from the interviewees, moving to just two feet (0.6 m) as the questioning continued. Then with the first group he moved to within a few inches of their faces, maintaining eye contact throughout. The result was that this 'severe crowding group' reacted very differently from the other. Their speech became disrupted and disorganized. Eye movements increased and gaze was averted. They adopted defensive body language, placing their arms and hands between themselves and the interviewer, and appeared much more nervous and restless than the other group. What this demonstrates is that personal space is very important to us and that insensitivity towards it, or misuse of it, can significantly affect the way we function.

Body orientation

Mehrabian calculated that over 90 per cent of the message in a face-to-face encounter is non-verbal, leaving less than 10 per cent for the verbal. This means that how you signal your intentions has less to do with what you say than how you come across to the other party. Much of this has to do with what is called **orientation**, which refers to the angle between two people and the direction they are facing. For example if you are sitting directly opposite each other, the angle is 0°. The further apart you are, the greater the angle of orientation between you.

A **symmetrical orientation** is when you are face to face, back to back, or similarly 'angled' towards each other. An **asymmetrical orientation** is when the angles are different, as when one person is facing directly, but the other is half-turned away. Asymmetrical orientations generally permit closer proximity than those which are symmetrical. Back-to-back orientations make communication difficult because without being able to see the other person's body language much of the message will be missed. As a general rule you can assume that:

- ▶ *the more direct the degree of orientation, the more attention is normally paid*
- ▶ *turning your back on someone will stop a conversation dead and is also rude*
- ▶ *facing someone, yet turning away to look over their shoulder, has the same effect*
- ▶ *being direct and open invites interaction; being closed and defensive doesn't.*

Curiously, when you are lying down (**horizontal orientation**) you tend to remember more than when you are standing up (**vertical orientation**). It appears that we are more imaginative and reflective when lying down, but less receptive to action, whereas we react more quickly and make decisions faster when standing, but are less responsive to new ideas or close examination of issues.

Where people choose to sit can tell you a lot about personal space and orientation. Think of the times you have been on a train or a bus and there are only a limited number of seats available. Do you just take the first seat that's free, even if it means sitting next to someone, or do you cast your eyes around to see if there is somewhere you can sit on your own? What about when you are going into a lecture hall? Do you immediately make for a seat towards the back, or go up to the front so that you can see and hear better?

Self-confidence has a lot to do with how we position ourselves informally and in public, but we don't always achieve what we set out to achieve. For example, individuals who go into bars in the hope of meeting someone they can talk to will often seek a seat in a corner from which they can observe. The problem with this is that if you hide yourself away you are sending the message that you don't want to be noticed. Far better to place yourself where you can be seen, preferably nearer to the action, such as at the bar where others may be doing the same thing.

If you sit with your back to other people, you make it impossible for face-to-face contact to take place. However, sitting directly opposite someone can initially prove to be as daunting for them as for you. Sitting at an angle offers a good compromise. By allowing indirect contact it enables you to make a quick assessment of the other person and offers the chance of opening up a conversation if desired.

The design of seating in public places counts for a lot. If you have square or oblong tables people who want to talk to each other will either sit diagonally across the ends, or directly opposite each other. People who do not wish to talk will tend to face in different directions or use the length of the (oblong) table to separate them. Albert Mehrabian suggested a zig-zag design for bar and cafeteria tables and counters, because he believed this would encourage people to interact better (see Figure 10.1). If seats are on swivels this also offers greater flexibility for making contact.

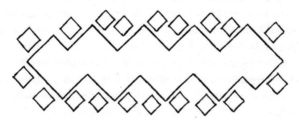

Figure 10.1 Mehrabian's zig-zag design for cafeteria tables.

You are what you project

How we use personal space and body orientation influences how we project ourselves and how we are received by others – in other words, **status**. It has been observed, for instance, that senior people align themselves to the right of whom they see as a leader, suggesting that the term 'right-hand man' has a basis in fact. Also people who sit at either end of the table in a jury room are most often elected Foreman – giving credence to the 'head of the table' notion.

In studies of office behaviour it has been found that people who perceive themselves as having low status tend to hover around the door before approaching a superior, whereas those of higher status have no hesitation in approaching the desk. Those who perceive themselves to be of equal status may come in and sit down next to their colleague's desk, while a friend may be greeted by the person whose office it is by coming out from behind the desk.

Competitive people tend to sit facing each other, while those involved in co-operative tasks will often sit side by side. There is no reason why you shouldn't place people opposite each other in formal meetings, though there is a greater tendency to **confront** when seated in this way. This is important when involved in negotiations. While traditional cross-the-table seating offers directness, round-table seating offers a greater sense of equality to all participants.

In interviews people tend to sit opposite each other and as far away as the size of the table will permit. Since the purpose of the interview is usually to obtain or provide information, the diagonal position at the corner of a table is preferable, particularly when only the interviewer and interviewee are involved. An informal setting is often more productive than a formal one, though job selection, performance appraisal and counselling require different approaches. For instance, sitting in comfortable chairs, perhaps with a low table in between, makes counselling, advising or sharing ideas easier. If you sit behind a desk or table you create a physical, and therefore a psychological, barrier. Formal assessment and appraisal, on the other hand, may benefit from such spatial distance.

Exercise 10: Competition versus co-operation

Figure 10.2 shows a table and six chairs. The 'X' indicates that a person you are about to meet is sitting there. What you have to do is decide which chair you would occupy in each of the following situations:

a *You are going to play a game of chess with this person and it is important for you to win. Place an A on the seat you choose.*

b *You are going to help the person complete a crossword puzzle. Place a B on the seat you choose.*

c *You are going to interview the person for a job in a small, friendly organization. Place a C on the seat you choose.*

Now, on Figure 10.3 place an X for the other person and an O for yourself on the seats you would consider most appropriate if you were going to conduct a formal disciplinary interview.

EXERCISE REVIEW

According to the research that has been done, you are most likely to have picked certain positions for each of the situations posed in the exercise. For a, you will probably have picked the seat immediately opposite the person against whom you were to play a game of chess. As we shall see later, we tend to sit opposite people we are competing against.

For b, you will probably have chosen the seat next to the person you were to help (that is, the seat to the right of the one marked X). We tend to sit alongside people if we are in a co-operative rather than competitive relationship with them.

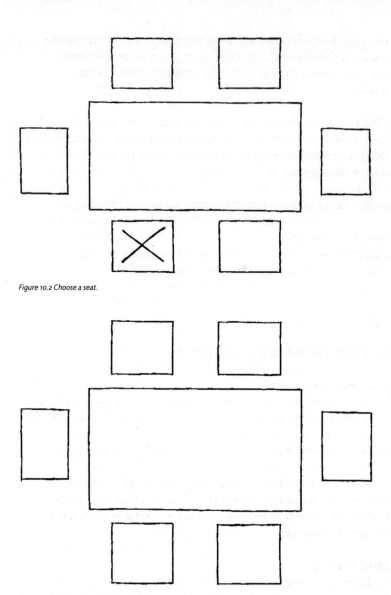

Figure 10.2 Choose a seat.

Figure 10.3 Position for a disciplinary interview.

For c, you probably selected the seat diagonally to the left of the person, at the end of the table. Diagonal seating arrangements have been shown to be particularly useful for interviewing situations.

When you were selecting positions for a disciplinary interview, the chances are that you placed yourself at the opposite end of the table from the person you were to reprimand. It is probably natural to want to distance oneself from what is likely to be an unpleasant task. It may, however, be that the diagonal seating arrangement used for other kinds of interviews may take some of the edge off the situation. Look at the exercise again and try to visualize the interaction that would take place in each possible combination of seats. Is one more formal than casual? If you're not sure at the moment, you may change your mind when you have read the next chapter.

Further exercises and experiments

Who's boss around here?
Try to observe a large open-plan office. See if you can determine, on the basis of how space is allocated and how people use personal space, who the high-status individuals are. Do they sit in some degree of isolation from the others? Do they have larger desks? Do they have more circulation space around their desks? Do they tend to sit at one end of the room or in the middle? What other territorial markers can you identify? How do others approach the desks of superiors? How do superiors coming in from other departments behave?

Lateral thinking
Lie down on a couch, sofa or settee and try thinking about what kind of day you have just had. After five minutes, stand up and continue your thoughts. Do you find it any easier to recall than when lying down? Then reverse the situation and see if it makes any difference.

Are you sitting comfortably?

Conduct an interview (as if, say, you were applying for a job) in the various seating arrangements suggested in this chapter. Which seems to be the most productive? If you cannot do this, watch some interviews on television with the sound turned down, and observe the use of personal space, territoriality and orientation. Which seems to progress most satisfactorily – the informal or the formal?

Come and talk to me

The next time you are in a bar, cafeteria or place where you often meet up with people, be aware of your personal space and orientation and see if it makes any difference in the way people interact with you. The easiest way will be to place yourself in or near to the centre of activity, though it might be useful to compare this with sitting on the periphery of events and observing the differences in other people's reactions.

11

Bodily contact

In this chapter you will learn:
- *about body contact and touching*
- *about the distinction between accidental touching and deliberate contact.*

Bodily contact is a highly sensitive area of body language and not something that should be treated casually. We know intuitively when someone does not welcome our touch, and it should be clear to all of us that if it is unwanted, we should back off. As we learned in the previous chapter, personal space has to be respected. As a rule of thumb, if you wouldn't tolerate someone touching you, then why should they tolerate you touching them?

Having the touch

Touch is one of the first of our senses to develop. Babies in the womb cannot see, smell, taste or hear, though they can experience sound vibration and touch. Once born, touch becomes a primary sense through which much of our earliest experience of communication is channelled. Haptics research has shown that where babies (and other young animals) are deprived of touching by others, their development can be stunted socially, emotionally and physically.

Touching can have a powerful effect on how we react to a situation. Even if we are touched accidentally or unintentionally, we can still be significantly affected by it. Mark Knapp reported an experiment in which a library assistant touched the hands of certain students – but not those of others – while library cards were being returned. Once outside the library, the students were asked to rate the assistant's performance. Those who had been touched, especially the females, judged the assistant (and the library) more favourably than those who had not. This was true both for those who were aware of having been touched as for those who were not.

Research shows that people are more likely to touch when:

- ▸ *giving information or advice than when receiving it*
- ▸ *giving an order rather than responding to one*
- ▸ *asking a favour rather than granting one*
- ▸ *trying to persuade rather than being persuaded*
- ▸ *at a party rather than at work*
- ▸ *expressing excitement rather than listening to someone else's excitement*
- ▸ *listening to someone else's worries rather than expressing their own.*

One study found that six out of ten people greeting or saying goodbye at an airport touched each other. As one might expect, longer embraces occur more frequently in departures than in arrivals. A number of studies have also found that touching is more often initiated by men than women.

To touch or not to touch

There is an important difference between bodily contact and touching. In the main, bodily contact refers to actions which are accidental, unconscious and made by any part of the body.

Touching, on the other hand, implies that the actions are deliberate, conscious, and made primarily, but not exclusively, by the hands. Michael Argyle has identified a range of ways in which these conscious contacts primarily take place (in Western cultures):

Type of touching	Parts of the body involved
Patting	Head, back
Slapping	Face, hand, bottom
Punching	Face, chest
Pinching	Cheek
Stroking	Hair, face
Shaking	Hands
Kissing	Mouth, cheek, hand
Licking	Face, arousal zones
Holding	Hand, arm
Guiding	Hand, arm
Embracing	Shoulder, body
Linking	Arms
Laying-on	Hands
Kicking	Bottom, legs
Grooming	Hair, face
Tickling	Anywhere

Richard Hedin places the various types of touching into categories ranging from very impersonal to very personal signals:

▶ Functional–professional *such as a doctor with a patient, a lecturer with a student.*
▶ Social–polite *such as handshakes and hand clasps.*
▶ Friendship–warmth *such as a friendly pat on the back or a shoulder embrace.*
▶ Love–intimacy *such as touching a loved one's cheek or a lover's kiss.*
▶ Sexual arousal *such as the mutual touching accompanying love-making.*

Desmond Morris identifies 12 steps which Western couples pass through on the way to sexual intimacy. Occasionally a step may be missed out, but they almost always occur in this order:

- *eye to body*
- *eye to eye*
- *voice to voice*
- *hand to hand*
- *arm to shoulder*
- *arm to waist*
- *mouth to mouth*
- *hand to head*
- *hand to body*
- *mouth to breast*
- *hand to genitals*
- *genitals to genitals.*

What these various kinds of touching mean depends on several factors, such as:

- *which part of the body touched the other person*
- *which part of the body is touched*
- *how long the touch lasts*
- *how much pressure is used*
- *whether there is movement after contact has been made*
- *whether anyone else is present*
- *if others are present, who they are*
- *the situation in which the touching occurs*
- *the relationship between the people involved.*

If you *deliberately and consciously* touch someone the response will depend upon how well you know the person. A stranger will react differently from a friend because knowing someone generally involves permission to enter their personal space. Touching implies a bond between the toucher and the touched, however, you can't assume that if you go around touching people they will necessarily like it.

Hands on

Handshakes are normally associated with greetings, farewells and cementing agreements. They can take many forms, spontaneous or formal, strong or weak, long or short, vigorous or mild, and indicate something about the nature of the encounter taking place. Most people in the West seem to prefer handshakes that are firm rather than weak, though in other parts of the world, such as Africa and the Indian sub-continent, gentler handshaking is the norm. Cultural differences need to be taken into account when judging the quality of a person's handshake. A gentler greeting does not imply weakness, insincerity or effeminacy – this is a curiously Western idea which links strength of handshake with strength of personality. Having a 'limp wrist' thus becomes a derogatory term associated with weakness.

Hand-holding Hands are also used for more prolonged holding than occurs in the handshake. Desmond Morris refers to these as 'tie-signs', or behaviours that indicate the existence of a special bond or relationship between two people. Whereas the handshake reflects a friendly greeting or a sign of respect, hand-holding indicates something more personal. Again, cultural differences influence attitudes towards hand-holding. Americans and western Europeans may raise an eyebrow at men holding hands, but in the Arab world such signs of affection are common amongst men and carry no sexual connotation.

Patting When the hands are used to guide someone in the direction you want them to go, light pressure is exerted on the person's back, arms or shoulders. Familiarly known as 'patting', this kind of gesture works only with those who permit its use. To do this without the acceptance of the other person may be regarded as patronizing, intrusive or even as unwanted bodily contact.

Stress reactions When people find themselves in stressful situations they often resort to touching their heads in some way. For example, drivers who are being 'tailgated' have been observed stroking their chins, grooming their hair, scratching their heads and eyebrows, rubbing their noses or the sides of their faces.

Intimacy

Embracing, hugging and kissing In some families overt signs of affection are a normal part of everyday life, in others they are rare. People who grow up in families where such familiarity is the norm tend to have better relationships than those where it is not. You can sometimes tell touchers from non-touchers by the openness of their gestures and a willingness to be embraced. Status factors influence displays of affection. While it is easy enough to hug and kiss a child, you wouldn't (normally) think of doing it to your boss or doctor.

Cuddling and tickling Those who enjoy physical contact and respond to it readily are less inhibited about touching and being touched. You tend to cuddle and tickle a child, or someone with whom intimacy is welcomed. In courting behaviour cuddling and tickling is often a prelude to sexual intimacy.

Stroking and caressing Stroking and caressing your own children is a normal part of demonstrating your love for them, though children approaching adulthood increasingly dislike being touched. In adulthood caressing is more often associated with sex. The more comfortable you are about your own body and about being touched, the more pleasurable you will find sexual intimacy – providing it happens by mutual consent. If it doesn't, it is unwanted bodily contact. The best advice is: when in doubt, don't touch.

Hands off

Aggressive behaviour often involves unwanted bodily contact. According to Michael Argyle, aggression is an innate response to attack, frustration and competition for resources. While it usually remains at the level of verbal threat, when provoked beyond our limits of tolerance it tends to spill over into physical violence. However, children fight, young men 'let off steam' by sparring with each other, lovers engage in sometimes quite forceful sexual activity – but in these cases the intention is not to cause harm.

In principle, uninvited or unwanted physical contact is a case of **hands off**. This isn't always that easy – as people (particularly women) on packed commuter trains will confirm. But you can't just lash out at someone who is crowding you. They may not have any choice since they, too, are being forced into contact with others. Better to turn your head and body away so that the immediate source of contact is indirect. This way you send a message that your personal space is inviolable.

Exercise 11: Who's touching whom?

Using drawings like those in Figure 11.1 in which the body is divided into various parts, conduct a brief survey amongst your friends and acquaintances to see where they allow other people to touch them. Try to ask an equal number of males and females. Ask them to identify the parts they would expect to be touched by their mother, by their father, by a same-sex friend, and by an opposite-sex friend. Record the responses on the figures by means of tallies (see Figure 11.2 for example). Make larger drawings of your own if this will help.

EXERCISE REVIEW

This kind of research was first carried out by Sidney Jourard and has been conducted by many others since. The results are nearly always similar. A typical set is given in Figure 11.2 and you should compare your own findings with them. As you can see, more people allow touching of most parts of the body by opposite-sex friends than by anyone else. The exception is the amount of touching of certain parts of the body permitted to mothers. Why do you think the same amount is not permitted to or expected from fathers? Why is there such a difference between same-sex friends and opposite-sex friends? Is the reason purely sexual? You might like to speculate on the answers to these questions as they involve taboo issues often ignored in family and close personal relationships.

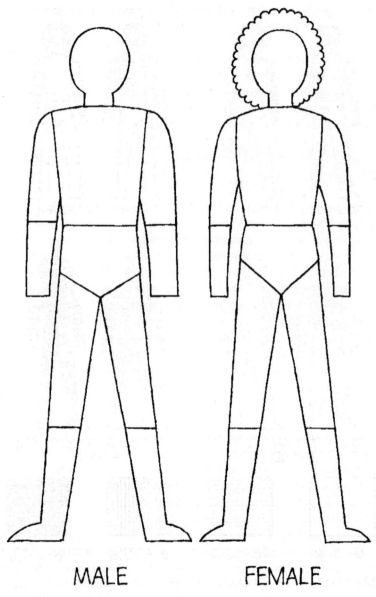

MALE   FEMALE

Figure 11.1 Where are you allowed to touch?

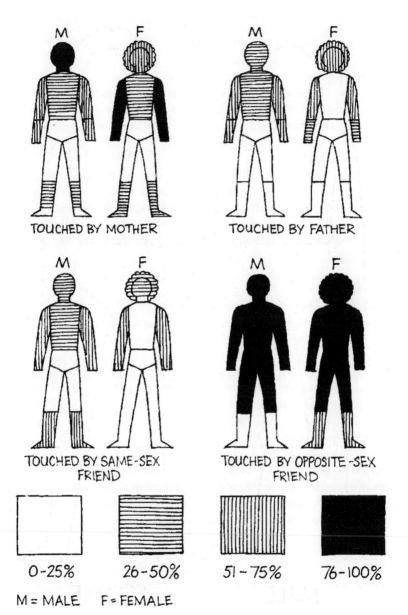

TOUCHED BY MOTHER

TOUCHED BY FATHER

TOUCHED BY SAME-SEX FRIEND

TOUCHED BY OPPOSITE-SEX FRIEND

| 0–25% | 26–50% | 51–75% | 76–100% |

M = MALE   F = FEMALE

Figure 11.2 Where people touch.

Further exercises and experiments

Don't touch me
In a café, restaurant, bar or other public place, observe people's touching behaviour. Try to identify the touchers and the non-touchers. What are the differences in their use of body language?

Give me a hug
The next time it is appropriate, hug someone whom you know well but whom you would perhaps not think it necessary to hug in order to communicate your affection for them. Examples might be mother, father, sister, brother, wife, husband or other close relation. What are your reactions to this exercise? What was their response?

Who is it?
Enlist the co-operation of one or two friends. Ask one of them to blindfold you and then direct you to another person. Try to identify that person by touching their face and head only. How easy is it to do this? Get the others to take it in turns to carry out the exercise. Discuss your responses to the activity. Can you find any general rules for identifying people by touch? How do people feel about being identified in this way?

Put it there
During the course of a day, try giving different kinds of handshakes to the people you meet. What are their reactions? Do you feel that people prefer a stronger or a weaker handshake? How do you react to the handshakes you receive from others? What is your own preference as far as handshakes are concerned?

Hang on
When you find yourself in physical contact with others whom you know well, try maintaining handshakes, hugs or kisses for slightly longer than usual. How do you feel about doing this? How do other people respond?

12

Shape, size and looks

In this chapter you will learn:
- *about appearance and physique*
- *how changing your appearance can significantly influence relationships.*

The shape and size of our bodies and the way we cover ourselves up exert a considerable influence over how others respond to us. You only have to think of the power of the fashion and slimming industries to realize how obsessed we are with our looks. What's more, we probably think we're in control of how we look.

There is no doubt that we go to a great deal of trouble to make ourselves presentable to the world. But why do we do this, and what do our looks have to do with body language?

Creating an impression

As we have already seen, our initial contact with other people is 'eye to body'; that is, we look at their bodies before we establish eye contact. This means that the first things we note are the clothes they are wearing, what these tell us about their body shape, and what we think about the impression they are creating.

Clothes adorn, protect, hide and advertise our bodies and have considerable communicative value in most cultures. They reveal something about our self-awareness, personality, income, status and occupation. We identify our age, gender, uniqueness or sameness through the way we dress and you can tell a lot about someone from their choice of clothes and the way they wear them. For example, introverted people tend to choose quieter or drabber colours, while the more outgoing go for brighter and contrasting colours. Even things 'thrown on' in the most hurried and casual manner can tell us a lot about how people feel about themselves.

But the pressure to 'look good' is always there. Generally speaking, feeling good involves looking good – which is why we put ourselves under pressure to find clothes that enhance our body shapes. How many times have you heard advice being given to wear darker colours for the lower part of the body and lighter ones for the top, and vertical rather than horizontal stripes to make you look slimmer? The point is that if you can disguise the bits you don't want people to notice, you feel more self-confident and create a better impression.

Appearance therefore provides useful clues to what people are like. Sales professionals and media people take a lot of trouble with their appearance because impressions matter. Sometimes they overdo it, appearing too smooth. The trick is not to appear too unconventional or pushy. Studies have shown, for example, that students are more likely to accept what a teacher says if he or she is dressed reasonably smartly and conventionally, rather than too informally. Even juries are influenced by appearance. Well-dressed, attractive women tend to get lighter sentences unless their crime involves something to do with their appearance – as in the case of confidence trickery.

Body confidence

If you don't feel good about your body you tend to communicate that to others non-verbally. Having a good physique obviously helps and there is no doubt that self-confidence emanates from a sense of being attractive to others. But being overweight, for example, shouldn't make you feel bad about yourself. What matters is that you are comfortable inside your skin; that you like yourself the way you are.

It is easier to change your appearance than your physique, but with increasing emphasis on health and fitness and slimming and dieting, men and women are going to great lengths to 'tone up' and reduce body mass. In an age when body consciousness dominates the advertising media we are forced more than ever to examine our shape, size and looks in relation to 'images of perfection'. Women are especially subject to this. You cannot turn the pages of a magazine these days without being shown how you could look 'if only...'

The effect of this is to make people judge themselves by comparison with images. If your hair, your skin, your teeth, even your choice of personal hygiene products, do not reflect what is 'in', you are made to feel like you are missing something. The fact that the actors and models who relay these messages to you are usually young and are chosen for their flawless complexions and perfectly toned bodies is rarely considered. Such is the power of advertising.

Going to such lengths to change the shape and size of your body is all about changing other people's perceptions of you and getting them to take more notice of you. Successful slimmers, for instance, often report an increase in self-confidence, a greater sense of well-being, and an improvement in their personal and social lives.

Body changes can also negatively affect your view of yourself. People who put on weight in middle age can become quite depressed, especially if they lack the will to do anything about it. Conversely, those who slim to the point of anorexia often have a poor self-image – believing that they are overweight even when, to everyone else, they look as if they are starving. This is because emotional and psychological factors sometimes get in the way. Not being able to stop eating, or just not being able to eat, suggest a negative state of mind. In such cases you need someone to talk to, to help get back on track and restore the balance.

Body shapes

We take for granted the fact that we identify men and women by
their body shape and looks. For example, men tend to be taller
and heavier than women. They have broader shoulders, smaller
pelvises, longer arms, bigger chests, lungs and hearts, stronger
skulls and sturdier jaws – and are therefore better protected against
physical attack. They also have deeper voices and more body hair
than women.

Women on the other hand don't grow beards, have softer skin,
slender waists, breasts, a wider pelvis (hence rounder bottoms)
and more of a hip sway when walking. The pelvis creates a
space at the top of the thighs – Desmond Morris named it the
'crotch gap' – as a sensible natural provision for their role as
child bearers.

You might well ask why, in this day and age, it is still just as
important to be able to detect gender differences. A lot of the time
it doesn't really matter. Androgynous males and females have long
been depicted in film and the performance media. Even in wider
(Western) society a blurring of sexual roles is tolerated. But while
the sex of the participants may not be that important in everyday
encounters, it is important in forming relationships, whether these
are straight or gay, and particularly if they are going to lead to
procreation.

We look for things in each other that we find attractive. This
doesn't mean that our choice of partner has to be a physically
perfect specimen, though it seems to count. Research has shown
that men who are taller than average are often considered to be
more intelligent and attractive, as are those whose body shape
is more muscular and fitter. Women whose bodies are slim and
curvaceous, emphasizing their femaleness, are often identified as
sexy and desirable by men because they (unconsciously) fit the
stereotype of the perfect breeding partner.

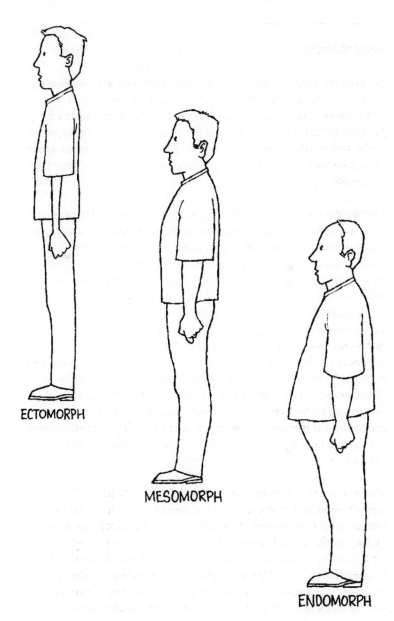

ECTOMORPH

MESOMORPH

ENDOMORPH

Figure 12.1 Body shapes.

Body shape also seems to play a part in how we respond to each other. A well-known classification, known as **somatotyping**, describes how body language associated with shape and size appears to influence our perceptions of character and personality:

- ▶ **Ectomorph** *Someone with a lean, low-fat physique and a high metabolism who has little difficulty in maintaining weight and body shape. Sometimes perceived by others as quiet and tense.*
- ▶ **Mesomorph** *Naturally muscular, with a trim waist and an equal ability to lose and gain fat and muscle weight. Often described as adventurous and self-reliant.*
- ▶ **Endomorph** *Someone with a heavy, rounded build, often with a marked tendency towards obesity or being overweight. Seen as being warm-hearted, agreeable and dependent.*

The ideal body

But how does this kind of body-typing square up to our perceptions of ourselves in the body image stakes? For a start, wherever you live in the developed world, the notion of the 'ideal body' crops up again and again. Fuelled by media images of 'perfection', young people in particular see themselves as too fat, too thin, too inadequate by comparison with their glossy role models and, as a result, unattractive. An Australian study which investigated the relationship between body shape preferences and eating disorders found that young women with high bulimic scores wanted to be thinner than what they perceived as being attractive. Their eating disorder problems stemmed directly from dissatisfaction with their own bodies and the search for 'perfection' – whatever that means.

In another study, a mixed group of Taiwanese undergraduates were asked to complete a body image questionnaire aimed at determining the meaning of the 'ideal figure'. The results showed that the men thought they looked almost exactly as they wished to see themselves, as well as how they thought women would wish to see them. By comparison, the women thought the ideal female figure was significantly thinner than their perception of themselves and the perception that others would have of their attractiveness. As well as this, the men overestimated, and the women underestimated, the body size they considered they needed to be in order to be attractive to the opposite sex. Whereas many of the men wanted to gain weight, most of the women wanted to lose it in order to arrive at their ideal shape. Ironically, the women preferred the men to be slimmer, while the men were happy with the women being 'more rounded'. When it came to 'the bits you like, versus the bits you don't', the men were generally satisfied with their body images, whereas the women were dissatisfied, citing the upper thighs and buttocks as their worst features.

The 'cost' to us of being preoccupied with body image is considerable. If you have preferred shapes and ideal bodies it means that a lot of people are going to be dissatisfied with what they look like and, consequently, how they feel about themselves. Worse still, failing to conform to images of perfection leads to discrimination – whether consciously or unconsciously applied – as well as self-exclusion. This happens when you start to be viewed, or you view yourself, as 'too fat', 'too thin', 'too tall', 'too small'... and find yourself being excluded from others' company.

According to Christine Craggs-Hinton, the social issue arising from our preoccupation with appearance is that we have less 'psychic space' to contribute to our wider communities. Many people, she argues, seem to care more about their appearance than about their 'growth as thinking people' – largely due to media emphasis upon achieving physical 'perfection'. At one end of the scale you have anorexics who are obsessed about putting on weight, yet constantly think about food. At the other end, you have people who are obese, actively rejecting calls to curb their dangerous eating habits.

The resulting preoccupation with self increases their intolerance of other people invading their privacy and personal space. Whether it is anorexia, bulimia, or compulsive over-eating, the underlying factors contributing to these eating disorders nearly always reflect negative feelings of self-worth, low self-esteem, poor body image and distorted self-perception.

Making the best of yourself

One of the paradoxes of life is that older people often try to look younger while younger people try to look older. Young men grow beards to look more mature, and balding men sometimes have hair transplants to make them look more youthful. Increasingly, women are having cosmetic surgery to enhance their best features and to 'delay' the ageing process. There's nothing particularly harmful in any of this, though trying to alter one's appearance suggests a lack of confidence, if not active dislike of who you are. The theory is that if others respond positively to such changes, you feel better about yourself.

The fact is that we can't stop the ageing process. We all change as we get older, but there are things we can do to slow these changes and to learn to avoid the factors which age us prematurely. For a start we can pay greater attention to diet and exercise and the damaging effects of smoking and alcohol. These are life choices. No one's telling you what to do. Most of it is common sense. The trouble is that an awful lot of us seem unable, or unwilling, to use it.

So what can you do to make the best of yourself? Why not try:

▶ **looking in the mirror** *or at recent photographs of yourself. Observe yourself in shop windows as you walk down a street. Get a friend to show you what you look like on a video. Build up a picture of yourself and set about making the changes.*
▶ **changing your clothing** *If you normally dress formally, try being a little more informal, or vice versa. If you habitually*

wear clothes of rather subdued colours, try being a little more colourful. Try experimenting a little with different kinds of clothing.

▶ **changing your hairstyle** *Colour, length, even hair extensions can make you feel quite different, and creating a new look can have an uplifting effect on your general confidence.*

▶ **slimming and taking exercise** *For a specified period, say, three months, such activities can dramatically alter your self-image and self-esteem. But don't overdo it.*

▶ **paying attention to face and skin** *Change your make-up, take note of new skin products, make sure you clean and moisturize your skin properly, get rid of unwanted or unflattering body hair.*

▶ **keeping up with trends** *Observe how other people dress and present themselves to the world. Ask yourself if you are doing everything to make the best of yourself. Don't copy, find your originality and show the people that matter to you that you matter to yourself.*

You don't have to go over the top. Just make up your mind what impression you want to make and set about achieving it. Your body language will tell others how good you feel about yourself.

Exercise 12: A complete change of clothing

The next time you go out socially, dress in an entirely different way from the way in which you usually dress. If you are in the habit of wearing smart clothes, dress very casually, or vice versa. What differences do you notice in the way your friends react? In the way strangers react? Do men react differently from women? How do you feel about dressing differently? Does it make you feel uncomfortable or is it a liberating experience?

You should have found, at the very least, that you can change your appearance and other people will tolerate it even if they may comment adversely. At best, you may well have found that a different style of dress enables you to interact more successfully with others.

Further exercises and experiments

Endo, ecto or meso?
What body type do you think you are – endomorph, ectomorph or mesomorph? If you do not fit a type easily, select the nearest one, or ask someone you trust, like a family member, to classify you. Then classify your family. Is there a predominant family type? Do you like what you see? Classify your friends. Do you choose friends who have the same body type as you?

Judging strangers
As you go about your daily business, observe the appearance and physique of other people. Speculate on their age, sex, status and likely occupation. What factors do you take into account in making your judgements? If the opportunity arises naturally, ask to find out how accurate you were.

Rough or smooth?
Try asking people for directions on how to get to somewhere when you are dressed very casually, then repeat the exercise when you are dressed really smartly. What differences do you notice in the ways people respond to you?

13

Time and timing

In this chapter you will learn:
- *the importance of time in Western culture*
- *about timing and synchronization as aspects of body language.*

Time and timing play a key role in non-verbal communication. The long pause, the quick-fire reply, the delayed entrance, talking and moving in unison – all reflect how we 'orchestrate' communication to suit our needs. Known as **chronemics**, the study of the use of time has revealed much about the way in which we interact with each other and how time affects communication between us. By improving our understanding and use of time we can not only become better communicators, but also manage our busy lives better.

More haste, less speed

We are obsessed with time in the West. We rush around at such a pace that we barely have time to think. Punctuality and scheduling dominate commercial life, and one's private life often has to fit around the demands of a job. 'Always looking busy' is seen as a way of impressing superiors, while working slowly and methodically is almost frowned upon. It's ironic that during the 1960s sociologists and planners were predicting a 'leisure society' by the year 2000 thanks to automation and the free time it was supposed to give us. If anything, we have less leisure time than before.

What we have to remember is that time is a finite resource. No matter how hard we try, we cannot squeeze any more than 24 hours out of any day. But what we can do is to make better use of the time we have available to us. The old adage 'more haste, less speed' sums it up very well. Hurrying simply leads to error. Instead we need to find ways of achieving our objectives without reducing performance.

Roughly a third of our day is spent asleep. Another third is spent working, and the final third is supposed to let us unwind and enjoy ourselves. The amount of time we spend communicating with others is actually very little. It has been calculated, for instance, that the average manager spends about a third of his or her working day communicating with others. By improving performance all round, time can be released, making it possible for more to be achieved in the space of time available.

Follow the rhythm

We all know there are times when we feel good and communicate well, and other times when we just want to be left alone. Often these feelings are influenced by the circadian rhythms of the body. These affect everything we do. When they are disrupted – for example, when you are jet-lagged – they can make you feel under the weather and lead to mistakes being made. It is at times like these that we are not at our best. This is why travellers crossing the Atlantic are advised to stay overnight at an airport hotel before driving on to their eventual destinations. After a good night's sleep the body has had a chance to adjust to a different time zone.

Some people find they operate better during the mornings rather than the afternoons. Some work best first thing in the morning, others later in the day. It doesn't really matter which category you are in as long as the 'larks' get their most important work done early and the 'owls' organize themselves so that the reverse happens. Studies of our ability to perform tasks suggest that we have 'highs' and 'lows', with mid-morning being best and mid-afternoon showing a noticeable decline in performance.

We have already seen how synchronizing body language with others can have a beneficial effect on encounters (see Chapter 8). Research has shown that we use eye contact, head nods, body movements and gestures in a far from random fashion. In fact, synchronizing with others produces a rhythmic pattern which some believe is essential to the success of communication.

The American researcher William Condon spent many thousands of hours undertaking a frame-by-frame analysis of films of people talking to each other and found that not only do those speaking move rhythmically, but so do those listening. Much of this rhythm isn't immediately obvious to a casual observer, but when slowed down the pictures show all kinds of minute changes of expression, eye movement, posture and gestures corresponding to the flow of the speaker's conversation.

Studies of eye contact have shown that there are distinct patterns of communication between people when they are getting to know each other. Adam Kendon observed that eye contact continues as one person finishes speaking, while the other person tends to look away before responding. If this does not happen, there is often a pause before the other person begins to speak. He also found that the listener's body movements tend to echo those of the speaker, showing that attention is being paid. Once the flow is resumed, whoever is listening settles back and displays little movement until that segment of the conversation draws to a close. A shift in position then signals that the listener now wishes to speak, and so on. Slowly, as rapport begins to build, the body language between the two develops its own rhythm. It is through these subtle changes in timing that the whole process of interpersonal communication is regulated.

Rhythm is also the essence of humour. Observations of comedians on stage show that timing is often as important as the gag itself.

They tease the audience with pauses and wait for the laughter and applause to die down before continuing, all the time holding their attention by keeping them in suspense about what's coming next. Poor tellers of jokes are the ones who fail to get the timing right. What this all means is that the non-verbal components of communication are just as important as the words themselves.

Silences and pauses

Silence doesn't mean that communication has ended. It can indicate a number of things. Pauses and short hesitations, for example, suggest nervousness on the part of the speaker, or moments in thought which aid delivery and maintain the flow of what is being said. The latter can be seen a lot on television where a pause gives a newsreader or reporter a moment to gather his or her thoughts. Not doing so makes the delivery seem rushed and lacking in confidence.

It's different in the case of chat shows and round-table discussions because interaction with others is taking place, rather than solely with the camera. Here the use of pauses and silences adds something to the discussions. By comparison, in police interrogations, silence can be interpreted as a refusal to speak, increasing the chance of being considered guilty. In other contexts, it may simply be a case of shyness, fear, or a lack of self-confidence making it difficult to respond.

Public speakers know that carefully chosen pauses can be used to great effect to wring either laughter or applause from an audience. Speakers at conferences will often indicate that they expect applause by pausing. This is particularly noticeable at a stage-managed political conference. Significantly, only high-status members of the party tend to make this technique work for them.

If you can, try recording yourself giving a speech or even simply engaging in conversation with someone. In this way, you can see how you use silences and pauses, how long they typically last and whether they occur in appropriate places. You may even be able to identify ways in which you can improve your use of silences and pauses when communicating with others.

Signalling your presence

Breaking into a conversation has its dangers. If you don't have the status to justify the interruption, the chances are that you will be ignored or told to go away. We unconsciously defer to those we perceive as higher in the social or organizational hierarchy than ourselves and it requires a subtle sense of timing to successfully gain their attention. Usually we do one of the following to achieve this aim:

▶ **Interrupt** *You have to be sure of your ground if you are going to do this. It isn't polite to interrupt and you may well be ignored.*
▶ **Raise the voice** *This may secure attention for long enough to enable you to make your point, but you can still be seen as being rude.*
▶ **Nod the head** *Single or double head nods signal that you are listening, but* triple *head nods signal that you want attention, or desire to speak.*

On the other hand, to show that you are willing to let someone else take over the speaking role in a conversation, you can simply:

▶ **pause** *at the end of a sentence, or finish off with a 'you know'*
▶ **end on a high note** *or drag out the final syllable*
▶ **maintain your gaze** *after you have finished speaking.*

If, on the other hand, you decide you don't want to speak, you can simply nod, grunt or make 'uh-huh' noises.

Making time work for you

If you want to make better use of time to develop your non-verbal communication skills here are a range of techniques which will help you to develop your own self-training programme – or flexible performance strategy. Try paying attention to the following:

▶ **Deadlines** *Make a record to see if you complete activities in the time allocated to them. By doing this you will begin to improve your performance and start to recognize where you have failed to make the best use of your time in the past.*

▶ **Increased flow rates** *Time an activity (e.g. reading) and then see if you can speed it up until you reach a point where it becomes uncomfortable to go any faster. You will then discover your optimum performance capability.*

▶ **Anticipatory scanning** *Before you undertake a task think ahead to the next stage and plan how you might aim to tackle it. For example, in airline check-in procedures, looking down the line for nervous or potentially awkward customers enables a skilled operator to anticipate problems before they reach them.*

▶ **Priority management** *Learn to identify the key features of a situation which seem more important, or relevant than others, and deal with them first. This way you learn to prioritize, thereby making better use of your time.*

▶ **Accurate feedback** *Keep proper records of your activities so as to avoid repetition and, therefore, time-wasting.*

▶ **Timing and synchronization** *Pick the best moments for moving into new situations and think about how to make a smooth transition from one to the next.*

▶ **Imagination vs. intuition** *Imagination is when you think you know. Intuition is when you know you know. You can save yourself a lot of time and effort by listening to your inner voice.*

▶ **Feel good factor** *Identify the times of the day (or night) when you are in the most productive frame of mind and use your 'high power' times to the maximum.*

▶ **Preserve down time** *Keep a 'reserve bank' of activities for spare time or odd moments when unexpected delays occur. This way you free up time for later on.*

▶ **Evaluate performance** *Study your records, analyse and evaluate how you have performed to see where further improvements can be made.*

Exercise 13: Performance enhancement

Select an activity such as reading an article, writing letters or reports, or walking from the station to the office, and time how long it takes to complete it. Then, over the course of the next week, do it again.

Each time, make a conscious effort to speed up just a little. Do not put any great effort into this, simply aim to achieve a new 'personal best' each time and see what happens. The important thing is to try to complete the task in slightly less time and to keep a record of these times. Try to ensure that tasks chosen are comparable in terms of size, length, difficulty and personal interest.

EXERCISE REVIEW

You should have found that you can speed up any activity without suffering loss of quality in performance. Sometimes the increase in speed can be quite substantial. In reading, for instance, it is not unknown for increases in speed of 100 per cent to occur without loss of comprehension. The average increase in speed is usually about 50 per cent. In writing, the possibilities for speeding up are more limited, but it you should still be able to achieve a saving of time on each letter or report of about 10 per cent.

If you have followed the instructions to the exercise faithfully you should find that you are capable of saving considerable amounts of time which you can now put to better use elsewhere.

Further exercises and experiments

Punctuality
To find out how the people you mix with feel about punctuality, ask them what time they would actually arrive for the following appointments and then compare them with your own time preferences:

- *a doctor's appointment at 9.45 a.m.*
- *a dinner date with friends for 7.00 p.m.*
- *a meeting with the boss at 2.30 p.m.*
- *an airline flight scheduled to depart at 11.00 a.m.*
- *meeting a friend for a drink in a pub at 7.30 p.m.*
- *an early morning radio interview to be broadcast live at 7.00 a.m.*
- *a blind date in a pub at 7.15 p.m.*
- *an interview for a job you really want, timed for 9.30 a.m.*

Time management
Take a sheet of A4 paper and divide it into rectangles so that you have a space for each half-hour of the working day from Monday to Friday. For two sample weeks, record in each space the main activity you have been engaged in. What proportion of your working day is spent in face-to-face communication with others? An example of a typical day's record is given in Figure 13.1.

Buying time
Over the next week, time your telephone calls and see if you can reduce them in length without appearing rude. What is the average length of call you make? What is the average length of call others make to you? What are the benefits? You should find that calls

can often be shortened appreciably without adversely affecting the quality of the communication which takes place.

Rapport

Observe other people talking, either around you or on television, and look for signs of poor communication. Examples could be both people talking at once, failure to synchronize, long uncomfortable pauses, or someone failing to get a word in edgeways.

Plan ahead

Remember what we said about anticipatory scanning? When you are under pressure, try thinking ahead and planning out how you are going to tackle the next part of the task. Anticipating what you are likely to have to deal with will save you time in the long run.

9	10	11	12	1	2	3	4	5

| MONDAY | Correspondence | Meeting | Telephone calls | Writing report | ″ | ″ | Lunch | Telephone calls | Meeting | ″ | ″ | Visitor | Correspondence | Writing report | ″ | ″ |

Figure 13.1 A simple time-planning exercise.

14

Signals and words

In this chapter you will learn:
- **about non-verbal aspects of speech**
- **why non-verbal signals such as pauses, 'ers', 'ums', changes in tone, pitch, pace and accent, can be just as significant as words.**

At the beginning of this book you were told that less than 10 per cent of what we communicate occurs during speech. It was probably hard to believe then, but now you know so much more about body language, you probably realize how much truth there is in the claim. We are so used to talking that we *assume* information is conveyed verbally. In reality non-verbal communication accounts for most of what we 'broadcast' to each other, so our signals are just as important as our words. Having said this, you may be just as surprised to learn that about a third of the information imparted during speech has less to do with words than sound and delivery.

Sounding good

We infer many things from the voice: age, sex, educational background, even attractiveness. Vocal characteristics enable us to make assessments of a person's character and disposition. For example, how often have you said 'he sounds nice to me', or 'I like the sound of that'? What you are actually doing is deciding whether you like or dislike, believe in or trust someone. The non-verbal aspects of speech form the basis of the study of **paralinguistics** and include volume, tone, pitch, voice quality, rate of speech, accent and stress.

▶ **Volume** *In order to inspire trust, volume should not be too high or too low. Trust is a two-way process. It is very difficult to trust someone unless you feel that they also trust you. Loudness gives an impression of a wish to dominate, which can militate against the development of mutual trust. A voice which is too soft gives an impression of diffidence or submissiveness, which also hinders the establishment of a relationship based on equality.*

▶ **Tone of voice** *should not be too harsh or too smooth. Harshness grates upon the listener and will tend to repel them. Too much smoothness can make them think they are having the wool pulled over their eyes and will make them suspicious. You also need to sound reasonably confident. It is difficult to trust someone who does not sound as if they trust themselves.*

▶ **Pitch** *Avoid shrillness in pitch. A voice pitched fairly low so that it has a soothing quality is more likely to be trusted. But don't overdo it.*

▶ **Voice quality** *If you sound nasal or breathless you are not likely to instil the kind of confidence in others that you are seeking.*

▶ **Rate of speech** *Fast talkers may think they are getting their point across because they are animated and persuasive, but they often give the wrong impression. The last thing you want in a trusting relationship is fast talk.*

▶ **Accent** *In the United Kingdom, people with regional accents tended to be discriminated against in the past because the notion of 'speaking properly' was class and education based. If you couldn't speak properly you didn't stand the same chance of getting a 'decent job' as those who spoke with a 'BBC accent'. Today this has all changed. Competence is no longer assessed on the basis of how you speak, but on how you perform, so don't worry if your accent is different from those around you.*

▶ **Stress** *Placing a little stress on positive words and phrases rather than on negative ones can lift a conversation and hold the* *attention of others more effectively. However, using too much stress, too often, can have the opposite effect. Like speaking too loudly, over-stressing certain points can give the impression of being 'mannered', or of wanting to dominate a conversation.*

Body words

The reason why non-verbal aspects of speech play a significant role in the body language of communication is because they:

▶ **add emphasis** *to what we are saying and meaning – as when we increase volume and rate of speech, or place stress on certain words and phrases. You need to be aware of how you sound as over-emphasis can result in over-statement. It's a bit like adding exclamation marks after every sentence. After a while they lose their impact.*
▶ **convey emotion** *Sadness tends to be characterized by low volume, a solemn tone, a deeper voice quality than normal, slower speech and uniform stress upon the words. Happiness and elation, on the other hand, are characterized by higher volume, sharper tones, a more breathless voice quality, faster speech and a more noticeable stress on key words and phrases.*
▶ **provide punctuation** *by means of head nods, gestures, changes of pitch and breaking eye contact. Except with questions, pitch usually falls at the ends of sentences and we use pauses to add emphasis to words and phrases.*
▶ **indicate nervousness or deception** *through speech errors such as mispronunciations, unfinished sentences, coughs, omissions, stuttering or stammering (where these are not a normal part of a person's way of speaking).*

Sometimes the words and expressions we use to describe how we feel actually echo our states of mind, providing verbal confirmation of what our body language is indicating. For example, we say that someone who is relaxed and comfortable with themselves is 'laid back', and someone who is depressed is 'down in the mouth'. You 'spit blood' when you are really angry, and you get 'jumpy' when you're nervous. You have 'a glint in your eye' when something's going well, and you're probably taking more than a slight interest when you 'eye-ball' someone. We utilize a wide range of such expressions every day without even realizing it. Here is a short glossary of a few more such terms:

Body language term	State of mind
in a cold sweat	anxious/afraid
squaring up to	confrontational
looking down one's nose at	superior
touching a nerve	irritated
if looks could kill	full of hate
that rings a bell	recalling
I hear what you say	non-committal
music to my ears	satisfied
curling the lip	aggressive
glazed expression	bored/confused
raised eyebrows	surprised/indignant
in the palm of my hands	manipulative/controlling
tight-lipped	protective/defensive
speechless	shocked
poker-faced	calculating
wrapped up in oneself	preoccupied
unable to stomach something	repulsed
I'm really touched by that	grateful
hollow-faced	empty/haunted
down in the mouth	miserable
seeing eye-to-eye	harmonious
feel it in my bones	certain
thick skinned	well-defended
pain in the neck	aggravated
to have your nose in front	confident
having considerable standing	respectful
bent	distrustful
lose face	lowered estimation

(Contd)

Body language term	State of mind
facts at your fingertips	authoritative
towering	powerful
upright	honest/dependable
taking a dim view of	critical
needing breathing space	claustrophobic

Ambiguous signals

If you say something, yet mean something else, it's quite likely that your body language will give you away. You may be deliberately setting out to deceive, or simply trying to avoid being direct, but either way, from the listener's point of view, there is a conflict between what is being said and what is meant. For example, you may hear someone saying positive things to you, yet find their tone of voice and body language extremely negative. Someone might tell you that they are very interested in what you are saying, yet be unable to maintain eye contact with you. You might find yourself smiling when you're actually thinking how much you dislike the person you are talking to. The danger is that, in all such cases, the signals you give are going to be picked up, and your honesty questioned. For these reasons it is important to be aware of your body language contradicting your words.

In politics and public life the use of ambiguous language is well known and widely employed as a strategy to buy time, promise support, but not necessarily to carry through with anything. Politicians, in particular, take great pains to conceal deception. It's not that they are less honest than the rest of us, it's just that political expediency often results in a lack of fit between promises and implementation. As we have already seen, the body language of deception involves all kinds of tell-tale movements which betray the intentions of the speaker. This is why media training is used to limit unwanted gestures, ambiguous signals and revealing personal habits. Get rid of signs of nervousness and uncertainty and you appear confident and upbeat. Astute politicians lean forwards to indicate a willingness to listen. They use more eye contact when they are speaking than is normal, because this makes them appear to engage with their audience and offers a better chance of controlling the interaction. They also try to have the last word in interviews because they recognize the verbal advantage gained by doing so and the non-verbal effect of being accorded 'higher status'.

Politicians also know that they need to be trusted. They will offer a firm, warm handshake to indicate commitment and openness; maintain eye contact and nod frequently to show receptiveness; moderate the pitch and tone of their voices to appear more sensitive to your needs; place a protective arm around your shoulder to demonstrate caring; and, above all, they will smile to display pleasure in meeting you. All this is necessary to create a favourable image for themselves, the party, and to maintain public support.

What's so funny?

Laughter is a non-verbal expression of amusement and usually accompanies smiles and grins. From the quietest chuckle or giggle to the most raucous belly laugh, it can be infectious, illuminating and even intimidating. When someone starts laughing it is often difficult to avoid joining in.

Though you might think that laughter is about lifting the spirits, it can also be used as a weapon. Essentially this is the difference between laughing *with* and laughing *at* somebody. When you laugh with others it is generally a spontaneous reaction to something funny, but when you laugh at someone you are deliberately setting out to poke fun at them. While this may be taken in good spirits by some, it can be wounding to others. If your *intention* is to humiliate or make look foolish, you need to ask yourself why you need to do it, as it could just be a way of hiding your own lack of self-confidence.

Exercise 14: Trust me

Try recording yourself to see if you convince either a friend or an imaginary stranger that you are to be trusted. You might pretend you are trying to persuade someone that something you have to sell is worth buying, that they should support you as a candidate in a local government election, or that you are talking a potential suicide down from a ledge. If you can enlist the participation of another person in this exercise, so much the better.

How do you set the volume of your speaking, the tone, pitch, voice quality, the rate at which you speak, your accent, and how do you place stress on the words you use? How does your use of the various non-verbal aspects of speech integrate with the verbal aspects or the words themselves? How successful do you think you have been?

If someone else is working on the exercise with you, you will be able to obtain this kind of feedback from them. If you are working alone, you will have to rely on your own best judgement when you play the recording back.

EXERCISE REVIEW

By this stage, if you have been doing the chapter exercises conscientiously, you should be noticing some improvements in your sensitivity to body language. If you have had reasonable success in conducting this exercise you may have noticed some of the following points:

Firstly, it's hard to persuade people, or sell to them, if you don't have the **confidence** to do so. Some people are naturally outgoing and therefore find face-to-face encounters relatively easy. This is why they make good sales professionals, media personnel and politicians. But many of us don't have this kind of confidence, so a degree of learning is required. Understanding the role of body language in communication is one of the steps towards making you a more confident performer.

Secondly, if you don't have any **experience** of face-to-face encounters you need to take time to increase your knowledge of what happens during social interactions. In particular, you need to **think about** what you are experiencing. This way you will gain a perspective on the role you are trying to perform. Just assuming that 'doing the job' will give you the experience you need is not enough. Without insight into the dynamics of performance, you are simply marking time.

Finally, you have probably realized from your recording that speaking into a microphone is a lot more difficult than it first appears. Just because media professionals, actors and pop stars seem to be able to do it effortlessly, doesn't mean you will. Once again, you have to **learn** how to control the volume, tone, pitch, stress, quality and speed of your voice. Once you have done it a few times it gets progressively easier. It is only when you listen back to what you have been saying that you recognize where you are at fault. Fluency in front of a microphone or camera takes experience, self-awareness and an ability to learn from your mistakes. Arrogance will get you nowhere. So don't start out thinking it's all a piece of cake, because your body language will betray you.

Further exercises and experiments

Er, ah, um
Select one or two public speakers, lecturers or speakers on television. Record the number and types of speech errors they make. Which is the one that each is most prone to make? You should usually find that nearly every speaker has a favourite speech error – 'er' is by far the most common.

Party political broadcast

Watch several party political broadcasts on television and see if you can identify the favourite facial expression, body movement, posture, and so on of each politician. Compile a list of typical non-verbal behaviours associated with each party. Compare and contrast them. Which parties are most similar to each other in styles? Which are the furthest apart? Is it possible to tell what a person's political opinions are likely to be from their body language?

Keep still

Using a recorder and standing in front of a mirror, record a short talk on a subject you know well. Try to make the talk without any body language at all. Is it possible? If it is, is it easy? You may very well find this exercise virtually impossible to carry out.

There's a call for you

Observe people on the telephone. How close is their body language to what it would be if they were conversing face to face? Which kinds of body language can be communicated by telephone and which cannot? Are any non-verbal behaviours more exaggerated when telephoning than in face-to-face encounters? Do any never occur?

15

Being a success

In this chapter you will learn:
- *that body language is key to your success as a communicator*
- *how understanding body language enhances personal growth.*

In 1859 the Scottish reformer, Samuel Smiles, published a book entitled *Self Help* dedicated to the notion of self-improvement through personal effort. He was one of those Victorians who believed that doling out charity to the poor was ultimately self-defeating because it offered no encouragement to people to 'improve their ways'. His ideas were eagerly snapped up in America and came to enshrine the principle of success through hard work and individual achievement. Today, the American 'self-improvement' market is estimated to be worth over $11 billion – roughly $36 for every man, woman and child in the United States.* That's a lot of investment in the business of helping people to help themselves.

***

Help yourself

In many achievement-oriented societies, making money comes at a price. The harder you work, the less you play – with the result that there just isn't enough time in the day for the 'ordinary

*Source: Marketdata. The US company estimated the self-improvement market to be worth $8.5 billion in 2003, with total market size growing to over $11 billion by 2008.

pleasures of life'. You often hear people saying they need to *make time* for these, as if relaxation, recreation and reflection come a poor second to the job. The danger is that if you live to work you see self-improvement in terms of career enhancement – with quality of life as a spin-off rather than a goal in itself.

Dale Carnegie's 1936 bestseller *How to Win Friends and Influence People* broke new ground in popular publishing on the subject of self-motivation. He showed how learning to communicate effectively is the route to success, but that it's down to you to make the effort if you want to succeed. This message has stood the test of time. 'Motivational' courses and programmes concentrating on self-development, personal growth and lifestyle management are extremely popular today, and are widely used in training and assessment. They echo Carnegie's (and Smiles's) belief that the desire to better oneself ultimately leads to the growth of self-confidence and, thereby, the improvement of personal performance.

Of course the downside of trying to be a success is that you also have to bear responsibility for failure. Personal growth isn't a one-way street. Overcoming bad habits and mistaken beliefs can be difficult, often requiring courage in facing up to the truth about yourself. But if you don't try, you never really know what you are capable of achieving. There's no use looking back on your life thinking what you might have been, if you haven't made the effort to find out what you're good at.

Winners and losers

In Chapter 4 we looked at styles of presentation and how these can be used to distinguish the wallflowers from the wolves in business situations. **Assertive** body language conveys confidence and gives the impression of experience and authority. When you seem on top of things, others accord you respect. Assertiveness can make you appear 'pushy', but if your body language is relaxed and informal, you come across as self-assured and sympathetic. This doesn't just apply to work situations, it applies to all walks of life. A 'winning way' is one which generates respect from others and an interest in who you are and what you have to say. If you remember, confident body language is characterized by:

- ▶ *upright, relaxed body posture*
- ▶ *direct eye contact*
- ▶ *open gestures*
- ▶ *relaxed facial expressions*
- ▶ *unambiguous hand signals*
- ▶ *a clear, confident voice.*

By comparison, **submissive** body language betrays feelings of inadequacy which may include:

- ▶ *quietness*
- ▶ *a nervous disposition*
- ▶ *slumped postures*
- ▶ *defensive gestures*
- ▶ *self-conscious behaviour.*

As we have already shown, there are many reasons why people lack confidence or feel inadequate. It may be that you were bullied when you were young, or simply that no one has ever made you feel good about yourself. But if you aren't encouraged by the people that matter in your life, what chance is there that you are going to feel like a winner in life? The more defensive, self-conscious, apologetic and self-deprecating you are, the more you attract unfair criticism and derogatory remarks. This can easily become a vicious circle. Once 'they' make you feel like a loser, you begin to believe you are a loser.

Self-motivation is what enables us to evolve into confident people, to be aware of our strengths and weaknesses and improve our performance. Understanding body language is a part of this. Being able to read the signals other people give us makes us better communicators. This way we present ourselves to the world as self-assured and believable.

What Carnegie did so successfully all those years ago was to pin-point the positive elements of communication that make people like us. He showed how to win others over to our own way of thinking, and to get them to change – without causing offence. For example, he emphasized the importance of being a good listener, of smiling, showing genuine interest in those you are dealing with, making them feel important, and putting them at ease. When you think about it, these are the same characteristics of non-verbal communication that we have been discussing in the foregoing chapters. Carnegie, like Smiles before him, may not have realized it, but he was laying the ground rules for understanding the role of body language in communication.

Nine golden rules

Adopting the same approach, we can now identify the range of body language skills that, if used properly, can ensure your success as a communicator. We'll call them the nine 'golden rules' of non-verbal communication:

1 **Make eye contact** *The more eye contact you make, the more you become aware of, and understand other people's intentions and meanings. To gaze indicates interest, but avoid staring. Remember, communication is as much a question of accurate reception as of skilful transmission.*
2 **Smile** *Lively and expressive facial expressions evoke positive responses from others, providing information about us which words cannot supply. Anyone can appear attractive if they smile.*
3 **Nod approval** *You express approval and indicate interest in others by using head nods. The more you encourage other people to talk, the more likely it is that they will trust and warm to you.*
4 **Open up** *Expressive gesturing that is neither contrived nor affected, suggests openness. Avoid defensive barrier gestures. Palms up, or palm-outward gestures convey a sense of welcome.*

5 **Look confident** *An upright posture suggests confidence and conveys active interest and involvement. Avoid stooping and slouching as these give the impression of sloppiness and lack of interest.*

6 **Don't back off** *In Western cultures we tend to distance ourselves more than in other cultures, so there are advantages in encouraging closeness. You soften stressful encounters by relaxing your body stance.*

7 **Touch with care** *Handshakes, hugs, pats, arm around shoulders and guiding hands on the arm or back suggest warmth, openness and a willingness to engage, but don't overdo it. Some may regard it as inappropriate, others as too forward. If in doubt, let the other person take the lead.*

8 **Good timing** *Be aware of the other person's body language and harmonize with it where appropriate, but do not deliberately copy it.*

9 **Watch your tone** *Avoid speaking too loudly, harshly or rapidly and keep the 'ums', 'ers', and 'ahs' to a minimum. Remember, tone of voice can be as important as the words themselves.*

Making an impact

We saw in Chapter 3 how important body language is in personal attraction. It can make the difference between hitting it off with someone and losing the chance to get to know them. The same applies in everyday social and work relationships too. If you want to make an impact, five factors that contribute to success are:

▶ *rapport*
▶ *empathy*
▶ *synergy*
▶ *self-disclosure*
▶ *charisma.*

Rapport is about making the other person feel comfortable with you. Successful communication depends upon it. To do this you need to recognize what you have in common and to work towards cementing bonds that can be relied upon in the future.

Empathy is the ability to experience a situation or problem from someone else's point of view. It involves the skill of relating to others by watching and listening without judging. Harmonizing your body language helps to make the other person relax.

Synergy is when you 'click' with someone and you don't have to say anything to know that you're getting on well together. Your body language does that for you.

Self-disclosure describes your willingness to volunteer information about yourself to others in order to convey a positive impression of who you are. It is best summed up as 'if you don't give, you don't get.'

Charisma is that extra quality which makes you stand out from the crowd and draws people to you like a magnet. We talk about charismatic people being *head and shoulders* above the rest, even *having us in the palm of their hands*. Charisma evolves with confidence. It's not just something you are born with.

End note

Winning or losing isn't really the issue. What you make of yourself is what matters. You are unique, which means that you have skills and abilities that others do not have. Being a success is relative. Comparing yourself to someone you regard as successful can either add a positive stimulus to your life, or make you want to give up. It depends on the baggage you are carrying. Too much and it will hold you back. This is why self-motivation is so important, and why developing your communication skills can make such a difference to your life. Body language skills, in particular, enable you to 'tune into' people's thoughts and actions, and play a vital role in supporting, or contradicting, spoken words. They also help you to monitor your own feelings, emotions and responses, making you more receptive and sympathetic to other people's points of view.

And as these skills continue to improve, so does your confidence. These are all steps towards fulfilling your true potential and enabling you to succeed in ways that you might not have done before.

Exercise 15: Rating body language

Now that you are a body language expert, try rating some of the key types of non-verbal behaviour to see how people match your assessments of them. For example:

▶ *While watching a chosen subject on television or in real life, record their body language on a coding sheet (see Figure 15.1). This can later be analysed for the purpose of establishing patterns and to identify peculiarities in behavioural styles.*
▶ *Record your own responses to your subject's body language on a rating scale (see Figure 15.2). This should provide further information for analysis and assessment.*

		e.g.	1	2	3	4	5	6	7	8	9
1	Eye contact	✓									
2	Facial expression change										
3	Head talk	✓									
4	Gestures	✓									
5	Posture change										
6	Space invasion/comfort										
7	Bodily contact/touching										
8	Looks, shape and size (scale 1 to 10)	8									
9	Timing and harmonizing	✓									
10	Ambiguous signals	✓									

✓ if behaviour present

Figure 15.1 Body language coding sheet.

attractive	_ _ _ _ _ _	unattractive
smart	_ _ _ _ _ _	scruffy
clean	_ _ _ _ _ _	dirty
self-assured	_ _ _ _ _ _	timid
ambitious	_ _ _ _ _ _	unambitious
warm	_ _ _ _ _ _	cold
approachable	_ _ _ _ _ _	unapproachable
popular	_ _ _ _ _ _	unpopular
happy	_ _ _ _ _ _	unhappy
calm	_ _ _ _ _ _	anxious
rewarding	_ _ _ _ _ _	unrewarding
generous	_ _ _ _ _ _	mean
sociable	_ _ _ _ _ _	unsociable
permissive	_ _ _ _ _ _	strict
kind	_ _ _ _ _ _	unkind
distinguished	_ _ _ _ _ _	undistinguished
respected	_ _ _ _ _ _	not respected
confident	_ _ _ _ _ _	unconfident
assertive	_ _ _ _ _ _	submissive
charismatic	_ _ _ _ _ _	uncharismatic
successful	_ _ _ _ _ _	unsuccessful
progressive	_ _ _ _ _ _	traditional
colourful	_ _ _ _ _ _	colourless
efficient	_ _ _ _ _ _	disorganized
extrovert	_ _ _ _ _ _	introvert
active	_ _ _ _ _ _	lazy
risk taker	_ _ _ _ _ _	cautious
impulsive	_ _ _ _ _ _	controlled
expressive	_ _ _ _ _ _	inhibited
responsible	_ _ _ _ _ _	irresponsible
pragmatic	_ _ _ _ _ _	reflective
relaxed	_ _ _ _ _ _	uptight
independent	_ _ _ _ _ _	dependent
tolerant	_ _ _ _ _ _	intolerant
bright	_ _ _ _ _ _	dull
masculine	_ _ _ _ _ _	feminine
straightforward	_ _ _ _ _ _	devious

honest	_ _ _ _ _ _	dishonest
open	_ _ _ _ _ _	closed
sensitive	_ _ _ _ _ _	insensitive
sympathetic	_ _ _ _ _ _	unsympathetic
considerate	_ _ _ _ _ _	inconsiderate

Place ✓ at point on scale, for example:
clean ✓ _ _ _ _ _ _ dirty
warm _ _ _ ✓ _ _ _ cold

Figure 15.2 Non-verbal behaviour rating scale.

Further exercises and experiments

Secret messages

There are many non-verbal games that you can play to help you develop your body language skills. Try enlisting the co-operation of family or friends, or if you are using this book as a class text, your fellow students. The first game involves the non-verbal transmission of messages.

Write numbers on pieces of paper sufficient for one to five players, fold and hand them out. Conceal the numbers from each other. Someone sits in the middle while the others make a circle around them. This person then calls out two numbers. The players with these numbers now have to change places.

The person in the middle has to take one of their places. Since no one knows anyone else's number, each player has to find out non-verbally who holds the numbers called – and do so without the person in the middle finding out.

If the person in the middle succeeds in taking a player's place when the changeover occurs then that player goes into the middle. The numbers are redistributed and the game begins again. It can be played until everyone has had a turn in the middle or until everyone is tired of it. No one may speak, except the number caller.

In playing this game, there are certain things worth looking out for. How, for instance, do the players establish who the numbered players are without the person in the middle finding out? Which aspects of body language do they use? How can the person in the middle best catch the non-verbal messages which pass between players? Is it more difficult to make others understand your number or to understand someone else's? How do players signal the moment when they wish to change places?

Sometimes a kind of conspiracy against the person in the middle can develop in which several players pretend to be the nominated numbers. This produces confusion and makes it easier for players to change places. You will find it useful to make a list of the things you learn from playing this and the other games in this chapter.

Random groups

A group of players moves freely around a room. A person appointed as the game leader calls out a number, such as two or four, and the players have to form into groups of that size. No one may speak. Anyone left over drops out of the game. The game continues until only two people remain. The aim is to see who the most successful players are by detecting differences in their use of body language.

Is a wink as good as a nod?

A group of players is divided into two halves. One half sits on chairs and the other stands behind them in a circle. One chair is left empty (i.e. there must be an odd number of players). The person behind the empty chair has to wink at a seated player. The seated player has to try to get to the empty chair and the person standing behind has to try to prevent him or her. If he or she succeeds in preventing the escape, both players change places and the person with the empty chair tries again.

The magic mirror
Each player finds a partner and stands facing them. The players try
to move in such a way that they copy each other, as if they were
mirror images. Those who observe the game should look to see
who gives a lead, which people are better at copying than others
and which people do things that are almost impossible to copy.

Silent drawing
A number of people sit around a piece of paper, supplied with
crayons or felt-tipped pens of different colours. No one speaks.
Each person contributes as much or as little as he or she wishes
to create a drawing on the piece of paper. Who starts? Who does
most? Who does nothing at all? How does the group decide it has
finished? What are the most common non-verbal behaviours?

Come in if you can get in
The players wait outside a room. They come in one at a time and
take up a position they find comfortable near people they like. No
one may speak. The game finishes when everyone is finally placed.
How many groups form? Who is left out? What body language do
people use to indicate that they want someone to join them? How
do they show they do not want someone to join them?

Conclusion

Body language is as important in communication as speaking, listening, reading and writing. In fact, it could be argued that it's more important given that less than 10 per cent of what we communicate to others is in the form of words. It is only relatively recently that attention has focussed on the non-verbal components of language and behaviour. Thanks to pioneering work across many disciplines – from zoology to paralinguistics – we know more about human communication today than at any time in our history. Research in chronemics, haptics, kinesics, proxemics and neurolinguistic programming has opened our eyes to this vibrant world of signals and cues, where hints, motives, intentions, feelings and judgements are transmitted through subtle gestures, signs and meaningful movements.

We use the language of the body to convey unspoken thoughts, and we take for granted that others will understand our meanings. Much of this happens at a subconscious level and we may not even be aware that our facial expressions, hand movements, winks, blinks, nods and sighs are sending out messages of affirmation, criticism, interest or dislike. The point is that language doesn't have to be in the form of words for meaning to be grasped by others. The way you use your body is like 'punctuation'. Without it, meaning and emphasis are lost.

It's only when we look more closely at our body language that we start to recognize what it is that makes us tick. Things we have missed in the course of our busy lives suddenly become evident. A smile, a raised eyebrow, a fixed gaze take on new meaning when the face is seen as the vehicle of unspoken emotions, unstated attitudes and hidden passions. A bowed head, folded arms, crossed legs and 'steepled' hands tell us whether we are succeeding or failing to convince. The way we stand, defend our personal space and allow ourselves to be touched sends a message about how confident we feel and about our willingness to interact with others.

We probably don't realize to what extent this 'silent language' endears us to people, how it opens or closes communication and makes or breaks relationships. This is because we don't consciously think about how non-verbal signals convey information about our state of mind during communication. But then why should we? We don't think about why we walk or talk either – we just do it.

Now you know so much more about body language you can begin to understand how it can improve your life. If you know how to read someone's facial expressions or their gestures and postures, you stand a better chance of interacting with them positively. 'Tuning in' to their actions enables you to interpret their thoughts and feelings, as well as making you more receptive to them generally. At the same time, your increasing awareness of your own body language helps you to present yourself in a more favourable light.

It's no good kidding yourself that presentation doesn't matter. How you look, how you conduct yourself in public, how you harmonize with others, even how you welcome and say goodbye – all influence the way in which you are judged by others. Attention to body shape and fitness and simple changes to appearance can have a significant effect upon how people respond to you. Being aware of the 'ums' and 'ers', the pitch, tone and pace of your voice, all contribute to the impact you make.

What it all comes down to in the end is how you want to be perceived. Being a success doesn't mean having to own a yacht, or being a TV celebrity, it has to do with self-respect and the desire to better yourself. Self-motivation is the key to personal growth, and the more skills you have at your disposal to achieve your full potential, the more successful you will become.

Hopefully, what this book has given you is the information you need to become a more accomplished communicator. By using what you have learned to increase your self-confidence and improve your performance, you will start to reap the benefits in your relationships, at work and in your everyday encounters with others.

References and further reading

If you wish to pursue your interest in body language, you may find it useful to read some of the books and articles below.

Argyle, M. (1972) *The Psychology of Interpersonal Behaviour*, Penguin.

Argyle, M. (1975) *Bodily Communication*, Methuen.

Axtell, R.E. (1997) *Gestures: Do's and Taboos of Body Language Around the World*, Wiley.

Birdwhistell, R. (1973) *Kinesics and Context*, Penguin.

Blake, A. (1997) *Body Language: The Meaning of Modern Sport*, Lawrence & Wishart.

Bok, S. (1980) *Lying: Moral Choice in Public and Private Life*, Quartet Books.

Carnegie, D. (1936) *How to Win Friends and Influence People*, Simon & Schuster.

Caro, M. (1994) *The Body Language of Poker*, Carol Publishing Corporation.

Clayton, P. (1999) *Body Language: A Visual Guide*, Newleaf.

Cohen, D. (1999) *Body Language in Relationships*, Sheldon Press.

Condon, W. and Ogston, W.D. (1996) 'Sound film analysis of normal and pathological behaviour patterns', *Journal of Mental Disease*, 143, pp. 338–47.

Cook, M. and McHenry, R. (1978) *Sexual Attraction*, Pergamon.

Craggs-Hinton, C. (2006) *Coping with Eating Disorders and Body Image*, Sheldon Press.

Cundiff, M. (1972) *Kinesics*, Parker Publishing Co (USA).

Darwin, C. (1865, republished 1965) *Expression of the Emotions in Man and Animals*, University of Chicago Press.

Duckman, D., Baxter, J.C. and Rozelle, R.M. (1982) *Nonverbal Communication*, Sage Publications.

Early, G. (ed.) (1998) *Body Language: Writers on Sport*, Graywolf Press.

Ekman, P. and Friesen, W.V. (1975) *Unmasking the Face*, Prentice-Hall.

Fast, J. (1971) *Body Language*, Pan Books.

Freud, S., edited by Strachey, J. and Freud, A. (1953) *Complete Works*, Vol VII, Hogarth Press.

Hall, E.T. (1959) *The Silent Language*, Doubleday.

Hall, J.W. (1999) *Body Language*, Harper Collins.

Harrison, R. (1974) *Beyond Words*, Prentice-Hall.

Hess, E.H. (1975) *The Tell-Tale Eye*, Van Nostrand Reinhold.

Jourard, S. (1971) *Self-disclosure*, Wiley.

Kendon, A. (2004) *Gesture: Visible Action as Utterance*, Cambridge University Press.

Kleinke, C. (1975) *First Impressions*, Prentice-Hall.

Knapp, M.L. (1972) *Nonverbal Communication in Human Interaction*, Holt, Rinehart & Winston.

Korte, B. (1998) *Body Language in Literature*, University of Toronto Press.

Lamb, W. (1965) *Posture and Gesture*, Duckworth.

Lambert, D. and Diagram Group (1999) *Body Language*, HarperCollins.

Lewis, D. (1996) *The Body Language of Children*, Souvenir Press.

Lovitt, J. (1996) *Body Language*, Lillenas Publishing.

Matthews, R.O. (1990) *Signs and Symbols: Body Language*, Wayland.

Mehrabian, A. (1971) *Silent Messages*, Wadsworth.

Mehrabian, A. (1972) *Nonverbal Communication*, Aldine Atherton.

Moran, R.T. and Harris, P.R. (1996) *Managing Cultural Differences*, Gulf Publishing.

Morris, D. (1967) *The Naked Ape*, Cape.

Morris, D. (1977) *Manwatching*, Cape.

Morris, D. (1979) *Gestures*, Cape.

Morris, D. (2002) *Peoplewatching*, Random House.

Neill, S. and Caswell, C. (1993) *Body Language for Competent Teachers*, Routledge.

Nierenberg, G.I. and Calero, H.H. (1973) *How to Read a Person Like a Book*, Hanau.

Quilliam, S. (1995) *Body Language Secrets for Success at Work*, Thorsons.

Ribbens, G. and Thompson, R. (2002) *Body Language in a Week*, Hodder & Stoughton.

Ribbens, G. and Whitear, G. (2007) *Body Language*, Hodder Arnold.

Robson, P. (1998) *Body Language*, F. Watts.

Rosenbloom, S. (2006) 'In Certain Circles, Two is a Crowd', Article in the *New York Times*, 16 November 2006.

Rosenthal, R. (ed.) (1979) *Skill in Nonverbal Communication: Individual Differences*, Oelgeschlager, Gunn & Ham.

Ruesch, J. and Kees, W. (1956) *Nonverbal Communication*, University of California Press.

Ruthrof, H. (1998) *The Body in Language*, Cassell.

Scheften, A.E. (1972) *Body Language and Social Order*, Prentice-Hall.

Shih, M. 'Body shape preferences and body satisfaction in Taiwanese college students', *Psychiatry Research*, Vol III, No 2–3, pp. 215–28.

Smiles, S. (1859) *Self Help*, London.

Sommer, R. (1969) *Personal Space*, Prentice-Hall.

Tiggemann, M. and Dyer, G. 'Ideal body shape preferences and eating disorder scores in adolescent women', *Psychology and Health*, Vol X, No 4, June 1995, p. 345.

Wiemann, J.M. and Harrison, R.P. (1983) *Nonverbal Interaction*, Sage Publications.

Wilson, G. and McLaughlin, C. (1996) *Winning with Body Language*, Bloomsbury.

Wilson, G. and Nias, D. (1976) *Love's Mysteries*, Open Books.

Zunin, L. (1972) *Contact: The First Four Minutes*, Talmy Franklin.

Index

Image credits